Conversations

About

Disciple

Making

Ken Adams

Day One:
"Where Have All the
Dawson Trotman's Gone?"

Years ago, I read a booklet by Dawson Trotman entitled *Born to Reproduce*. This booklet is about being fruitful and multiplying disciples in your life. While I enjoyed reading it, the thing I really want you to focus on is the fact that I read it "years ago."

What saddens me is I have not seen very many books about multiplying disciples published in the past several decades. Imagine how God must feel when the thing so close to His heart is not being written about or discussed among His children. Yes, I have purchased and read a few books on discipleship but not many on disciple making. From time to time an author comes along who writes a book on spiritual disciplines or spiritual growth, but where are the books on multiplying disciples? I'm not talking about *adding* disciples but *multiplying* them!

What I am about to say next is the reason I am writing this book. As I study the life of Christ, His plan to reach the world through multiplication becomes very clear to me. Yes, Jesus came to redeem mankind back to God, but His chosen method to do so was by multiplying disciples.

Look at what Jesus said just before He left earth in Matthew 28:19-20, *"Therefore go and make disciples of all nations, baptizing them in the name of the Father and of the Son and of the Holy Spirit, and teaching them to obey everything I have commanded you. And surely I am with you always, to the very end of the age."* Jesus pulls no punches, and He makes it very clear that He left His disciples here on this earth to make more disciples. We are not here just to grow deeper, to have great worship, and to experience warm fellowship. You and I are here on this earth to multiply disciples of Jesus Christ!

So how are we doing? Is God's church a movement of multiplying disciples? Perhaps a better question is, "How are you doing?" How many generations of disciples are the results of your intentional efforts? I know few mature Christians who can point to multiple generations of disciples in their lives. In fact, I know very few Christians who have personally led someone to faith in Christ, much less helped someone else come to the point where he or she has led someone to faith in Christ. Are we really born to reproduce? Did Jesus commission us to multiply or not?

I am writing this book to help you learn how to multiply the life of Christ in others. Over the next ninety days, I hope to motivate, inspire, and educate you on how to reproduce generations of Christ's disciples. This book will be a success if it equips you to become a multiplier for Jesus Christ. I will try to pick up where Dawson Trotman left off and attempt to show you that you really are here to reproduce disciples.

If disciple making was the very thing Jesus counted on to reach the world, one would think that libraries and bookstores would be full of books on disciple making. I think God is honored that you are reading this book. Let's start with the very thing Jesus came to do—multiply disciples!

Day Two:
"Jesus' Family Tree"

A number of years ago, my uncle decided to trace the roots of the Adams family. Now be careful. I know exactly what you are thinking. Uncle Fester is not in my family tree! Anyway, my uncle dug and dug and actually came up with an amazing picture of the family tree from which my family descended. I had no idea I was related to the second President of the United Sates. I still have no idea if I am a relative of John Adams, but I thought I could make you think I was. It worked, didn't it?

All foolishness aside, do you ever wonder about your ancestors? Do you ever think about who had some contribution in you being here? I think about my family tree from time to time, but I hardly even remember my grandparents much less my great-grandparents or especially my great-great-grandparents. All I know about the majority of my ancestors is that their last name was Adams.

I wonder if anyone in my family tree ever once worried about populating the world with Adams'. I wonder if there was ever an Adams who was concerned with producing multiple generations of our family. I doubt it. I doubt seriously that we ever had an Adams who gave much thought to more than one or two generations of family. I think all the Adams' of the past simply focused on multiplying one generation. If my great-great-great-grandparents did the right things with the next generation, everything else would take care of itself.

This is the very concept Jesus used. Jesus had a family tree that started with the original twelve disciples. Jesus obviously thought about populating the world with disciples, but He only focused on the next generation. If Jesus did the right things with the first generation of disciples, everything else would take care of itself. Jesus only had to equip one generation of disciples to become reproducers, and if they did the same thing with the second generation, a global movement would begin.

You and I are part of Jesus' family tree. The original disciples didn't think much about us; they simply focused on passing the baton to the next generation of disciples. Slowly but surely, despite ourselves, the discipleship lineage has lasted more than two thousand years. The real question we must answer today is this: are we doing the right things today to ensure another generation of disciples will be reproduced tomorrow?

Jesus has commissioned us to make disciples of all nations; however, the only way to reach all nations is to start with a handful. Are you living your life in such a way that the baton will be successfully passed to another generation of disciples? My experience tells me that many mature Christ followers live their entire Christian life and never multiply one disciple. Is that what Jesus had in mind? We cannot possibly reach all nations if we are not willing to multiply Christ in others.

Why not accept the challenge to invest in a handful of disciples today? Make time in your life to meet with a few potential disciples and pour the life of Christ into them. If you do this well, they will in turn do the same thing with someone else. Over time, there will be multiple generations of disciples who have long forgotten you but know Jesus very well. Isn't that why we are here?

Jesus' family tree made it to you; make sure it doesn't stop with you. Pass on the life of Christ to others!

Day Three:
"A Man Named Clete"

Several years ago I had lunch with a very interesting individual. His name was Clete, a campus minister at a major college a few hours drive from where I live. The thing that made Clete so unique was his vision. I had never met a man who had a vision for multiplying his life as this man had.

During a very casual, get-acquainted lunch, I asked Clete where he was headed in life. I kind of expected him to say something about retiring and settling down. You know, the "cruise 'til the end" mentality. I was not expecting to hear, "I plan on spending the rest of my life influencing a million men for Jesus Christ."

Wow! I tried not to drop my fork or my jaw, but Clete's vision totally took me off guard. I had never met a person who had such a clear, concise, and calculated plan for reproducing disciples of Jesus Christ. As I probed deeper, he explained that his goal was to personally disciple a handful of college-age men for as long as he could, and those men would multiply themselves all over the world if he did his job the right way. He figured that over time, through multiplication, his life could influence well over one million men. How many people do you know who even have those kinds of thoughts?

A few years after this lunch conversation with Clete, he went home to be with the Lord after battling a rapidly growing form of cancer. The good news is Clete is in heaven, and his influence for Christ is still going!

The key to Clete's vision is the exact same thing we see in Christ's life—intentionality! Jesus was intentional about His investment in a handful of men. He was not "winging it" while He was here. Jesus was strategic. He selected twelve men who could pass on to others what He had given them.

Jesus was intentional about who He was, what He said, and what He did. He wanted His disciples to follow His model. Jesus wanted His disciples to demonstrate His character and values. Jesus was intentional when He spoke to His disciples only what God the Father wanted Him to say. He made His words count, and with His words, He imparted the truth of God. Jesus was intentional in what He did. The disciples saw

Jesus reach out to the lost, pray, and withdraw for solitude. They saw Him speak to the multitudes and then reserve time just for them. Jesus was not "winging it"!

So, how intentional are you? Do you, like Clete, have an intentional plan for multiplying your life through others? Are you strategically modeling for others the same way Jesus did? In 2 Timothy 2:2 Paul told Timothy, *"And the things you have heard me say in the presence of many witnesses entrust to reliable men who will also be qualified to teach others."* Once again, that is the intentional life. Paul told Timothy to be strategic by picking the right kind of men and giving them what he had received from him. In turn, they were to go out and give it to others.

I know very few people who live their lives with such intentionality. I bet you know very few either. Isn't it amazing that we hardly know anyone who is doing exactly what Jesus did, and what Paul told Timothy to do? Why don't we change that? Like Clete, no one knows how long we have to live. Let's make the most of what time we have left, and multiply the life of Christ.

Day Four:
"The Last Day at Chick-fil-A"

Every Friday at 6:00 a.m. for almost fifty-two weeks, I met with three other men from our church at the local Chick-fil-A restaurant. We met for two reasons: accountability and fellowship.

Our weekly meetings were great. You may be wondering how anything can be great that early in the morning. Well, after a cup or two of coffee you would be surprised how many good things can happen when God shows up in the middle of a small group.

Week after week, we poured into each others' lives. We challenged each other to be better husbands and fathers. We pushed each other to meet regularly with God and serve in ministry. We asked each other the tough questions about life and encouraged each other when things were not going so well. We enjoyed each others' company and forged a really tight group.

All was well in our little booth in the corner of Chick-fil-A until Jesus started convicting me. Like a linebacker leveling a running back, He leveled me with some hard-hitting truth about our group: Jesus did not come just to produce great fellowship. Jesus came to produce multiplying disciples.

Yes, fellowship is important. Jesus used fellowship as a major part of the growth environment for His disciples, and fellowship is a part of the process of making disciples. However, fellowship is not the end result of the disciple-making process!

The more I learned about the life of Christ, the more I realized our group could not continue as we had been. Sure, we could keep meeting in that booth each week, feel good about ourselves, and stay comfortable. However, we could not do that and still be true to the model Jesus had given us. In John 20:21 Jesus said, *"Peace be with you! As the Father has sent Me, I am sending you."*

If Jesus had come for the sole purpose of producing deep fellowship and accountability, you and I would not be following Him today. The whole movement of Christ followers would have died out shortly after Jesus left planet earth. The Father did not send the Son just to create deep fellowship groups. The Father sent the Son to start a movement of multiplying disciples who would do exactly what the Son had done. We will fellowship with one another for all of eternity, but we only have one shot at reaching this lost world for Jesus Christ.

I believe the best thing that ever happened to our men's accountability group was coming to grips with what Jesus had been sent here to do. The realization was hard for me, but I had to break it to our group. I remember the Friday morning when I told them I could not continue meeting with them in the same way we had been meeting. I told them I loved the fellowship and accountability, but I could no longer justify having another venue of fellowship without also having a place for multiplication to take place in my life. I said they could continue meeting without me, but that I needed to move out of the group so that I could invest my life in a few more men. I wasn't sure how they would respond, but I had no choice. I could no longer justify this two-hour block of time spent in this way. I had plenty of fellowship in my life already, but I had no reproduction in my life at all. How could I be doing what Jesus sent me to do if I had no time for multiplying disciples?

The last day at Chick-fil-A was bittersweet. The fact that I was giving up a great time of fellowship with three good friends was bitter, but our next meeting with twelve men gathered in a room at Shoney's ready to become good friends was so sweet. I still have a certain level of fellowship with those three guys I met with in the corner booth, but that last day at Chick-fil-A was the first day of something even better. It was the first day of a movement of multiplying disciples.

Day Five:
"From Four to More Than A Hundred"

I will never forget the excitement in that small room in the back of Shoney's restaurant; it was contagious. The four of us who had met at Chick-fil-A had not only changed eating establishments; we also changed our focus. Each of us had decided to get intentional about reproducing disciples for Christ. All four of us prayed and invited two to four other men to join us in a small-group discipleship environment. Each week about fifteen men gathered for breakfast, a brief large-group devotion, and then small-group growth time.

The fellowship in that back room of Shoney's was so rich; we could have met there every week until Jesus came to take us home. We could, but we would not have been true to what Jesus called us to do—multiply!

At the end of a year, the small groups in the back room knew what needed to happen. We all knew we needed to multiply. Not every group reproduced; however, some did, and the next thing you know we had about twenty-five men crammed into that small room at Shoney's. It was awesome! Can you picture it? A room packed full of men sharing, learning, and praying between 6:00 and 7:30 every Friday morning.

I loved two things about meeting at Shoney's—the breakfast bar and the fellowship. We could have met in that back room 'til Jesus came back. We could have; but we couldn't keep meeting there and ever become a movement of multiplying disciples.

When we outgrew the room at Shoney's, we decided to move our men's discipleship time to another greasy-spoon restaurant called Shirley's. We actually had to ask Shirley, the owner, to open up for breakfast and allow us to have the whole place to ourselves. She agreed, but it only lasted two weeks. Shirley and crew just could not make the 6:00 breakfast happen. When Shirley closed the door on us, we moved the meeting to our church and brought in biscuits. It was great!

I still remember the first day all our groups invited new men to attend. We were now over fifty strong at 6:00 on Friday mornings. Can you picture fifty men coming together for a short time of worship then breaking out into small groups for a discipleship study and accountability time? This was a great time of growth for the men in that group. Many of those men are now leaders in our church. Life change was taking place right before our eyes every week. We could have met like that for years. We could have, but we would not be a movement of multiplying disciples.

Over time, we decided to reach out to the men who could not make the 6 a.m. start time. I mean, why penalize a guy for being too lazy to get out of bed in the morning? Actually, many of the guys who joined our first Tuesday night group were already at work when our Friday crew was pouring their first cup of coffee. This was a great new growth environment. Every Tuesday night we had thirty to forty men showing up for worship and small group growth time. The environment was electric, and we did not even have food!

The Friday morning and Tuesday night groups included more than one hundred men involved in small group discipleship. Watching a movement of multiplication blossom right before our eyes was awesome! We could have kept meeting like this for years; but we had to keep multiplying. We actually decided to decentralize our groups and abandon the large group times. To this day, small groups of men are still popping up in restaurants and in our church building on any given day of the week. I've lost track of the number, but the end result is still taking place. At times, I feel like this resembles the way the church grew in the New Testament. The first words of Acts chapter 6 seemed to be true for us, *"In those days when the number of disciples was increasing..."*

Day Six:
"From Newnan to LaGrange"

Jesus gave the disciples orders to be His witnesses in Jerusalem, Judea, Samaria, and to the ends of the earth. They did okay with the Jerusalem part, but they had a little trouble getting motivated to take on Judea. In Acts 8:1, we see a little incentive given to get the gospel out of Jerusalem. *"On that day a great persecution broke out against the church at Jerusalem, and all except the apostles were scattered throughout Judea and Samaria."*

The scattering of the church in Jerusalem tells me that God can do whatever He chooses to get disciple makers wherever He wants them!

God's ability to move disciple makers anywhere He wants them is exactly what happened to Tim, one of the three guys who met with me on Friday mornings at Chick-fil-A. Tim had been comptroller at a car dealership in downtown Atlanta for a number of years when he found out the dealership was closing. As Tim began interviewing with other car dealers, he came across a Christian, Chris, who owned a dealership south of Atlanta in the small city of LaGrange. The two men hit it off right away, and Tim went to work for Chris. Tim lives in Newnan, and now drives forty miles south to LaGrange each day rather than driving forty miles north to Atlanta.

When Chris hired Tim, he not only got a top-notch accountant, he also got a top-notch disciple maker. Chris did not know it at the time, but Tim is actually a disciple maker disguised as an accountant.

Shortly after starting to work at the new dealership, Tim invited Chris and a couple other men to join him in a discipleship group using Impact materials. God really began to work in the midst of this group. All of these men experienced life change and caught God's vision for disciple making. They began to realize they were created to be and build disciples of Christ.

When Tim and his band of brothers in LaGrange completed the Impact course, they decided it was time to multiply. Imagine that! Tim caught the vision, and over the course of a few years, the number of disciples going through Impact in LaGrange had grown to nearly one hundred.

Tim invited me down to LaGrange a couple of times to attend a

men's Impact campout. You wouldn't believe it. These campouts had
about fifty men standing around a campfire telling their God stories. It
was amazing how God worked when a handful of men met to discuss
the Scriptures, pray, and hold each other accountable. The Impact course
was simply a tool to get men together in a life-changing environment.
The campouts also served as recruitment times for more men to jump
into a discipleship group. Over time, many of these men's wives decided
to join the act, and today hundreds of men and women in a small town
called LaGrange are reproducing disciples of Christ.

I think it is only a matter of time before God moves someone in
LaGrange to another part of the world to multiply more disciples. God
has a way of putting us where He wants us. The main question is this: Do
we know why God has put us where we are? At first glance, you might
think God put Tim in LaGrange to count dollars at a dealership. I believe
God put Tim in LaGrange to make disciples. Why has God placed you
where you are? I don't know what type of work you do, but I do know He
put you where you are to make disciples who make disciples!

If God moved disciple makers from Jerusalem to Judea and Samaria,
then He can certainly move them from Atlanta to LaGrange. Never
underestimate what God can do, and never underestimate whom He
will use. God's plan is that people just like you and me are to be His
witnesses in Atlanta, Newnan, LaGrange, and the ends of the earth.

Day Seven:
"Every Member a Multiplier"

All the guys in the LaGrange discipleship group call my friend Tim, "Pastor Tim;" I find this quite humorous. They joke about Tim being the pastor of the Impact Discipleship movement that is spreading throughout this small town. Tim can't stand it when they call him their pastor, and of course that just makes them do it even more. I've even been guilty of poking fun at his "Holiness" a time or two.

Have you ever thought about the fact that some of the things we joke about are actually the very things God wants us to be about? The more I study the life of Christ, the more I have come to realize that Christ wants every disciple to be a disciple maker!

When Jesus gave us the Great Commission, He did not say, *"Go make disciples of all nations if you have the gift of teaching or leadership."* No way! Jesus knew there could not be a global movement if His disciples only mobilized a few gifted leaders to do the job. Jesus knew that a global movement of disciple making would require every member of the movement to be a multiplier.

I know what you are thinking, and you are right. Not everyone who comes to Christ is automatically ready to multiply other disciples. Babies don't have babies. Even teenagers are not fully equipped to have babies. Becoming a disciple maker takes time. Even Jesus spent almost three years equipping His team of multipliers. Every member is automatically an evangelist, but it takes a little time to equip every member to be a multiplier. In Mark 3:14 the Scriptures tell us, *"He appointed twelve— designating them apostles—that they might be with Him and that He might send them out to preach."*

Jesus used the "with Him" time to equip and train His team of multipliers. They walked with Him and watched His life as He modeled for them how to live. The disciples caught a great deal from their teacher. They listened to His teachings. They saw His character on display. They did ministry with Him. They became what He was—a member, a missionary, a minister, a magnifier, a multiplier. Every disciple needs to be equipped so that eventually he can be sent out!

So where are you? Are you in the "with Him" stage, or are you in the "sent out" stage? Are you at the place in your spiritual development where you still need to be equipped for multiplying, or are you at the place where you are ready to start multiplying? I don't know your stage of spiritual development, but I do know that there should be many more multipliers in the movement. In thirty-plus years of walking with Christ, I've only met a handful of people who have multiplied more than one generation of disciples. Why don't we have more members living as multipliers?

I could write several chapters on why I think we have a shortage of multipliers in the harvest field. Here are just a few of my conclusions.

First, many disciples want life-long learning. I know some believers who spend their entire spiritual journey wanting to go deeper. They go deeper and deeper but never go wider. Jesus never intended His disciples to go so deep they get muddy! Yes, Jesus wants His disciples to keep growing, but part of the growth process comes from passing truths on to others. If I had waited until I knew everything there was to know about being a father before I had a child, I would never have become a father.

Secondly, many disciples believe they have been equipped to do something else other than disciple making. Jesus did not take the disciples "with Him" to equip them to do programs, or to stay busy until He came back. Jesus equipped His disciples to make more disciples. You cannot get around this issue. If you study the life of Christ, you will see that Jesus made disciples to make more disciples. He did not make disciples to make busy Christians.

Finally, many disciples are convinced someone else will do it. So many people have been led to believe that only the "pastor" can make disciples. Hogwash! In Greek, that means *hogwash*. Jesus never said, *"All you Pastors, go make disciples!"* Jesus commissioned all of His disciples to make disciples. That includes you! Do not wait for Pastor Tim to move to your town. Start a movement of multiplication today.

Behind all of these conclusions is one common denominator. The enemy is against multiplication. In fact, I believe the enemy will concede a few movements of addition just to keep true multiplication from happening. Satan will attack multiplication because he knows how powerful it can be. Don't let Satan keep you from being a multiplier. Remember, every member is called to be a multiplier!

Day Eight:
"The Master Plan ... Really?"

Go into the study of any pastor and you will find a copy of Robert Coleman's classic book, The Master Plan of Evangelism. With less than two hundred pages, this book is the classic work on the way Jesus made disciples. The title itself suggests that multiplying disciples is the God-given strategy for global evangelism. This book is a must read. Get a copy today and read it, or ask your pastor if you can borrow his. I'm sure he'll be more than glad to loan it to you.

One of the things I find interesting is how many pastors have Robert Coleman's book, but how few have more than one generation of disciples in their life. I am even amazed at how many pastors go through their entire ministry and never have one small discipleship group in which they invest time. How can the leaders of the church not be doing the very thing Jesus came to do?

I remember having a conversation with a pastor who said, "You don't really believe we can reach the world by reaching two people, and they reach two more, and on and on, do you?"

I said, "Actually, I do. I believe that is the model Jesus gave us, and if we work His plan, the plan will work."

He went on to say he believed satellite television was the best resource we have for reaching the world for Christ. That's funny; I don't remember Jesus saying anything about making disciples by satellite. Imagine how hard that would have been for the original disciples.

My goal is not to pick on pastors. I do think pastors ought to be leading the way for the church, but my goal is to stress the fact that a multiplied life is the God-chosen plan for global evangelism. Whether pastors make disciples or not, the fact remains that God sent Jesus Christ to multiply His life! Following Christ's model is the best way to reach the world.

Think about it. If we had a world filled with multiplying disciples, we could reach an incredible number of people. The "each one, reach one" concept really could produce a global movement of evangelism if we simply stayed focused. Check out what Jesus said in John 14:12, *"I tell you the truth, anyone who has faith in Me will do what I have been doing. He will do even greater things than these, because I am going to the Father."*

Wow! Jesus packs a punch in that statement. Notice that He indicates one of the evidences of faith is doing what He did. What did He do? He made disciples! Jesus came to redeem the world, and set in motion a movement of multiplication so everyone could hear the message of redemption. The evidence of faith is not a televised program across the globe via satellite.

Jesus also claims that anyone who does what He did will accomplish even more than He did. How can that be? We can accomplish more than Jesus did simply because we have more time here on this earth to multiply than He had. Jesus had less than three years to invest His life in a way that would be reproduced. Many of us have seventy to eighty years to invest our lives in a way that will outlast us. Do you think God's heart breaks when some believers live their entire lives and never even attempt to do what Jesus did?

I believe God's heart is grieved by our lost focus on disciple making. The vision drift that has occurred over the past two-thousand years is unbelievable. Somehow, the enemy has successfully caused us to forget the focus of the Master's plan. We celebrate our additions while the enemy chuckles at our lack of multiplication.

Maybe we ought to do more than read a copy of Robert Coleman's classic book, The Master Plan of Evangelism. Maybe we ought to do it! Making disciples who make disciples is the Master's plan.

Day Nine:
"The Apprentice"

A number of years ago I took on the task of building my own house. I was considered the general contractor even though I had plenty of help from several builder friends. During this process, I learned quite a bit about building a house, and also about building a disciple.

One of the experiences I remember most from building my house was the time I hired a man to build columns on my front porch. I hired a well-recommended brick mason to come in and do the job. The job was completed, but the man I hired did very little of the work. In fact, most of the time he sat in his truck or ran errands while his apprentice did the work.

I remember the day I asked him how long he could get this young guy to do all his work for him. He laughed, and then began to explain to me the process of development I had not been able to witness. It went something like this. The young man, who served as his apprentice, or journeyman, was his nephew. He started working for him four or five years earlier as a helper. During that time, he did a lot of digging, mixed a lot of mortar, and watched as his uncle laid the bricks. In time, he hired another man to do the digging and mixing, and he began coaching his nephew in the fine art of masonry. During this stage, his nephew got hands-on training and worked alongside his uncle to learn the trade. Now by the time they started working on my house, a new phase of development had begun. The apprentice was doing most of the work while the master mason was watching. The young apprentice would soon start his own business and leave the supervision of his uncle.

I don't know if my brick mason or his nephew has plans to train additional masons, and I doubt they have plans to start a global movement of brick masons. If I had to guess, I would say masonry is a family trade and that another family member had taught the uncle how to lay bricks. My hunch is that they will keep passing on the trade as long as someone in the family wants to learn.

By now you can see why I said I learned a lot about disciple making while building my house. My brick mason gave me a perfect picture of what Jesus did with His disciples. I have a new frame of reference for what Jesus said in Luke 6:40, *"A student is not above his teacher, but everyone who is fully trained will be like his teacher."*

In the same way a master mason trains an apprentice, Jesus trained His disciples. Jesus wanted His disciples to be "fully trained" before He sent them out to train others. He wanted them to watch what He did. Jesus wanted them to learn what He did alongside Him. He wanted to watch them do what He did. Jesus wanted them to go out by themselves and do what He did, and He wanted His disciples to train others to do what He did. That is disciple making!

Have you ever thought what a tragedy it would be to have a world without brick masons? I doubt you have ever lost sleep over it, but it is possible. It is possible that the art of masonry could die out. If all the master masons decided to stop training apprentice masons, it would only be a matter of time before finding someone to do brickwork would be next to impossible.

I don't have any doubt that someone will continue learning the art of masonry. There is a big enough need for brickwork to keep people learning the trade. As long as a master mason takes the time to train an apprentice, the workers will be there.

Heaven forbid that masons try to teach masonry by any other means than apprenticeship. What would the world be like if masonry was taught on-line, by correspondence, or in lecture halls? What would happen if students spent their whole lives learning the skill of masonry but never walked alongside a master mason? What would happen if individuals could earn diplomas in masonry but never really touch a brick or mix mortar?

Heaven forbid that disciples of Jesus Christ ever try to make more disciples by any other means than apprenticeship. What would happen if disciple making were condensed to nothing more than passing information from one student to another? What would happen if application ceased to exist? What would happen if young disciples never watched mature disciples do ministry? What would happen if young disciples never walked alongside mature disciples? What would happen if experienced Christ followers never mentored growing Christ followers? What would happen if fully trained disciples never intentionally invested in untrained disciples? What would happen if we got so busy building ministry programs, we forgot to build disciples?

I hope you lose a little sleep over these questions. Better yet, I hope you wake up and find an apprentice to train. Heaven forbid that disciple making would lose steam on our watch. The need for disciple makers is constant. Will there be enough workers for the need?

Day Ten:
"The Ultimate Growth Experience"

Everywhere you turn these days people are talking about the ultimate this and the ultimate that. We seem to be living in a culture that wants the maximum rather than the minimum. We want the ultimate ride or the ultimate thrill. We want the ultimate game. You name it, and we want it as long as it is the ultimate.

I often wonder, however, how many people are searching for the ultimate spiritual growth experience? How many people are willing to position themselves in an environment that is going to stretch and grow them like never before? I am afraid not too many people are longing for that experience or even know what it is.

Before I became a parent, I had no idea how much I was about to grow. No one told me that being responsible for three children would stretch me in ways I never imagined. Even as I am writing now, I am thinking about a decision concerning one of my children for which no one ever prepared me. There is no way I could have known all there is to know about parenting before becoming a parent. I often find myself thinking about the statement people make, "I never realized how much my parents went through until I became a parent."

If you wait until you are totally prepared to be a parent, you will never become a parent. A big part of learning to be a parent can only be experienced by being one. Once you take responsibility for someone else's well being and development, you will be surprised at how much you learn.

Making disciples is the ultimate spiritual growth experience; you will never grow more than when you are assisting, under the direction of the Holy Spirit, in the growth and development of a younger believer. Helping a new or young believer grow in his or her faith will stretch you in ways you have never dreamed. Just try it. You'll see.

Please do not make the mistake so many people make. Do not wait until you are fully prepared to help someone else grow because you will never be fully prepared! Nor do you want to make the mistake of thinking that the ultimate growth experience is the accumulation of more knowledge. Gaining greater amounts of information does not necessarily mean you are experiencing maximum spiritual growth. Yes, we do want to be life-long learners, but a major part of life-long learning is life-long teaching.

As a pastor, one of my responsibilities is to teach our congregation God's Word in the adult worship service. I have been doing this for a number of years, and I can tell you that every time I teach, I learn the most. Any teacher will tell you they grow more by teaching others than they do by being taught.

I did not wait until I knew it all before I started teaching. There was a point where I knew enough to begin teaching, but I have learned more by teaching than I would have ever learned had I waited until I knew it all. Even Jesus did not give His disciples all they could possibly know. He simply gave them enough so they could do what He had commanded them to do. Jesus said in John 7:33, *"I am with you for only a short time, and then I go to the One who sent Me."* In the short time Jesus had with His disciples, He gave them enough knowledge to disciple others. He knew that once His disciples started making disciples, they would continue growing as disciples. Jesus gave His disciples the ultimate spiritual growth experience by commissioning them to make more disciples.

How cool is that? Have you ever thought about the fact that Jesus was setting His disciples up for life-long learning by calling them to be life-long teachers? My question for you is quite simple. Are you a life-long disciple maker? The answer is either yes or no. If you answered yes, congratulations; you are well on your way to the ultimate in spiritual growth. If you answered no, what are you thinking? Don't you want ultimate spiritual growth? Now you know how to get it, so go for it.

Day Eleven:
"Wrong Number"

Don't you hate to be in the middle of something important when the phone rings only to discover someone dialed the wrong number? Even worse is to be sound asleep and get the same type of phone call in the middle of the night. Why would someone be calling another person at that time of the night anyway? Thank the Lord for Caller I.D. At least now, I do not have to worry about missing a call from a phone number I recognize.

I often feel that we, as believers, are concerned with the wrong numbers. Numbers are important. There is even a whole book of the Bible called Numbers. God certainly wants us to keep track of important things by using numbers. God has given us numbers to help us evaluate how well we are accomplishing His mission. We count people because people count.

Using numbers to track people and measure our mission is not bad as long as we are counting the right numbers. I can only imagine how frustrated God gets when we give Him the wrong number.

A newsletter I receive in the mail each month is a perfect example. This newsletter is a denominational paper that gives lots of news and information regarding this particular denomination. It also gives regular reports on the progress of certain churches. The two primary reports featured in this paper are a report on giving to the denomination, and the number of baptisms by leading churches.

I can see the importance of tracking baptisms. At least that is one part of what Jesus told us to do in the Great Commission. The amount we give to the denomination is another story altogether. I won't even bother writing about that issue. I often wonder, however, why this newsletter never reports the one thing Jesus came to do: make disciples! Why doesn't this denomination give a report on how many disciples are being trained and sent out? I have been involved as a church member for over forty years, and I have never known a church that reports on how many disciples their members have multiplied. Could the lack of such a report be an indicator of the fact that multiplying disciples just is not happening?

Maybe we do not report multiplication numbers because Satan has lulled us into accepting addition. What would it look like if the churches that baptize three to four hundred people were reporting meager results in multiplication? Do we really want to know the state of affairs in the church today? Are we ready for the truth about our efforts to multiply disciples? I honestly believe we have the wrong numbers.

We need to track several different numbers to evaluate our success in accomplishing the mission Christ gave us. We need to track baptisms, giving, and visitors to our church services. However, we must also evaluate how many disciples we multiply.

I suggest the tracking start with you. I recommend that you keep a personal record of how well you are doing at multiplying disciples. Keep a list or chart in a journal or in your Bible of whom you have helped to disciple, and who they have gone on to help disciple. If you keep such a record, you will be in a very elite group of people. You can search near and far, and you will only find a small remnant of disciples who are committed to a lifestyle of personal multiplication.

The desire of my heart is to leave behind a long list of disciples who have gone on to disciple others. In fact, I hope the impact of my life will be so great I cannot track it all. Don't you think this is the way Jesus intended for all of us to live? Don't you think He wanted all of His disciples to be multiplying disciples?

How are you doing at living a lifestyle of personal multiplication? Are you staying the course and consistently investing in other disciples? Or have you gotten distracted and lost sight of the one thing Jesus came to do? Is it possible that you have settled for a life of personal addition rather than personal multiplication?

God is in the middle of something very important. He is trying to redeem the world. I hope I don't send God a wrong number. That can be very frustrating, can't it?

Day Twelve:
"We Call It the
Great Commission for a Reason"

When I graduated from seminary, I was sent out by my
denomination to serve as a church planter. My objective in ministry
was to start a new church and give leadership as it grew into a mature
congregation. Before I began this new ministry, I participated in what
my denomination's mission board calls a Commissioning Service.
During this service my wife and I, along with several other couples and
singles, were charged with the calling of starting a new church. The
focus was very clear. We had not been commissioned to start a school,
a hospital, or a homeless shelter. All of those are good things to do, but
they are not what our denomination was sending us out into the world to
do. I clearly knew that I was being commissioned to start a new church.

More than two thousand years ago, Jesus Christ conducted a
commissioning service. He gathered His disciples on a mountainside and
said, *"Go and make disciples of all nations, baptizing them in the name
of the Father and of the Son and of the Holy Spirit, and teaching them
to obey everything I have commanded you."* With these words, Jesus
sent His disciples out into the world. Their focus was very clear. They
were being sent out into the ministry fields to make more disciples. The
original disciples were not sent out to start schools, construct hospitals,
or build houses. All of these are very good things, and they can be used
as ways to help make disciples. However, they were not the reason Jesus
was sending them out into the world.

The words Jesus spoke to His disciples two thousand years ago
are the exact same words He is saying to us today. His words have
not changed in all that time. Jesus is still commissioning us to make
disciples! He has charged us to go into the world and make disciples
who will make even more disciples. The focus is very clear. We can
use schools, hospitals, or other ministry concepts, but we had better
be making disciples who multiply disciples. How tragic it would be to
make sick people well, but not help them become disciples. How sad it
would be to educate thousands of people, but not develop a multiplying
movement of disciples. How heartbreaking it would be to build everyone

a house, only to see those houses become wood, hay, and stubble while souls miss a home in heaven.

I'm really not trying to be hard on people who build schools, hospitals, and houses. I thank God for anyone who loves God and serves people. My whole goal is to remind us of our focus. Jesus made it extremely clear. Make disciples! Let all of our efforts come back to the making of disciples who look like Jesus Christ. Anything less than this objective is a waste of time.

We all need to remember that we call Jesus' charge to make disciples the Great Commission for a reason. Jesus did not want us to get distracted. He did not want us to lose our focus or get so busy with things that we forget the main thing. Jesus made it so simple. He told us to go. He told us to baptize. He told us to teach all that He had commanded. In a nutshell, Jesus expects us to make disciples who will turn around and make more disciples. If we stay focused on this calling, we will eventually make disciples of the whole world.

So how are you doing? Has your life been focused on the Great Commission? Have you been effectively investing in making disciples who make disciples, or have you been too busy to make disciples? Are you distracted and focused on other pursuits? You can turn things around. You can realign your priorities and focus your life on what Jesus commissioned you to do. Remember, we call it the Great Commission not the Great Suggestion. Jesus did not commission us to make disciples if we had time for it. He commissioned us to make disciples because the world is dying and going to hell. That is the reason we call Jesus' charge to "make disciples" the Great Commission.

Day Thirteen:
"Dividend Disaster"

I barely remember her. We called her Aunt Maggie, and she lived in central Florida. I remember my family going to see her once or twice while on vacation during my childhood years. She was actually a great aunt on my mother's side of the family. I do remember that for some reason, she placed my brother and I in her will. When Aunt Maggie died, she left us several shares of stock in AT&T and Southern Bell. I can certainly understand why she left stock to me, but why she left any for my older brother is still a mystery!

Over the past thirty or so years, I have received quarterly dividend checks of a few hundred dollars. I have never actually added it up until now, but my best guess is that I have received around ten thousand dollars in dividends during that time. I've spent those checks on a number of different things, none of which were very important or essential. The one thing I did not do was reinvest those checks. Today, I often wonder how much stock I would have if I had reinvested all those dividends for the past thirty years! I can only guess that my stock value would be far greater than it is today. That is a real bummer!

When speaking on disciple making, I often ask people if they would rather have $100,000 right now, or have a penny a day and double the amount every day for thirty days. You would be surprised how many people want the hundred-grand right away rather than taking the time to let multiplication happen. If you accepted the one hundred thousand dollars in one lump sum, you would give up a little over ten million dollars gained through the power of compound interest. That is a dividend disaster!

This example of compound interest is a perfect picture of how we settle for adding disciples instead of multiplying them. I'm afraid we want the short-term results rather than the long-term payoff. Finding a person who has led a few people to Christ is easier than finding one who has trained anyone to lead people to Christ.

When you look at the results of Christ's ministry, at first glance you might not be very impressed. At the time He left planet earth, He did not have a large following. He had drawn crowds of thousands, and He had an influence that spread to tens of thousands; however, He only had 120 committed followers when He appeared to them after the resurrection. In 1 Corinthians 15:6 Paul says, *"After that, He appeared to more than five hundred of the brothers at the same time, most of whom are still living, though some have fallen asleep."* Compared to the following of many ministries today, Jesus did not seem to have a mega-ministry.

However, appearances can be deceiving. If you look at the following Jesus has built over the past two thousand years, the numbers go well into the billions. No one I know has had that kind of ministry following. Jesus blows away the concept of mega-ministry when you view His fruit over the long haul. The principle of multiplication becomes very clear by the way Jesus lived His life. He was relying on this principle for reaching the world. He knew the limited potential of addition, and the unlimited potential of a movement of multiplication.

If Jesus lived by the principle of multiplication, why would we not live by the same principle? I wonder why most believers I know have settled for a life of addition rather than one of multiplication? Are we so focused on the short-term gratification of decisions that we are not willing to go for the long-term satisfaction of multiplying disciples?

Don't stop reaching people for Christ. Go after the lost at all cost. However, make an equal commitment to multiply disciples who will go after the lost at all cost. Think multiplication, not addition. Aunt Maggie would be proud of you, and you would have a lot greater investment in the Kingdom.

Day Fourteen:
"Make Disciples, Appoint Leaders"

If there is a buzzword in the Christian world these days, it has to be ... "Leadership." Everywhere you turn, someone is talking about the importance of raising up Christian leaders. Leadership books are in great supply, and leadership CD's and DVD's are big sellers. Leadership conferences are drawing people by the thousands. A look at the Christian community lately would lead one to believe the answer to all our problems is developing more leaders.

I want to be the first to say that leadership is a huge factor in the spread of Christianity. A movement will only expand as quickly as its leadership expands. My question, however, is simple. How are we developing individuals to become leaders?

Every year for the past several years, I have attended a very large church leadership conference. Each year the pastor stands up and reaffirms his commitment to bringing the best and freshest leadership material he can to this inspiring event. He is a champion of the leadership value. I applaud his effort, and I learn a great deal about leadership from his teaching and influence. I do, however, leave this conference every year wondering, "Where is the conference and the person championing the value of making disciples?"

As I understand the ministry of Jesus, it appears to me that He came to make disciples rather than leaders. Once Jesus had made mature disciples, He appointed them leaders. He did not come to make leaders; He came to make disciples who would be ready to take on the responsibility of leadership. In Mark 3:16 the Scriptures say, *"These are the twelve He appointed..."* Jesus appointed to leadership individuals whom He had trained and equipped. Jesus made leaders out of mature disciples. Jesus certainly did not appoint people to leadership who had not first proven to be trained disciples.

Why, over forty-plus years of being in church, have I seen countless numbers of people appointed to leadership positions who were not first proven mature disciples?

When I was in a College and Career class, I had a Sunday school teacher who had been divorced three times and went through his fourth divorce while teaching the class. He actually stopped teaching as his divorce took place. That does not seem to me to be the leadership development plan Jesus had in mind.

A friend of mine told about a member of his extended family who went through a divorce while teaching a Sunday school class and no one in the church even knew it had happened. Where is the accountability in this leader's life?

I believe, with all my heart, that the movement of Christianity needs more leaders. The church will not expand without them, but I also believe that we will never have enough leaders if we don't make a priority out of making disciples. Where will the quality leaders come from if we do not have a process in place to develop qualified prospects for leadership?

The leadership pipeline Jesus used was discipleship. Jesus took seekers and turned them into servants. Jesus took fringe followers and developed them into fully trained leaders. Jesus helped people in the crowd find their way into called positions of ministry. Don't you think we ought to be doing the same thing?

How would you like to stand before Jesus some day and listen to Him read a list of names of people who became spiritual leaders because you helped disciple them? If we had a huge pool of disciples to choose from, appointing leaders would be much easier. Why not commit yourself to helping build that pool. Why not live as a champion of the Great Commandment and Great Commission. If you invest your life making mature disciples, think how many leaders you might have helped to develop.

Day Fifteen:
"Seeds in an Apple, Apples in a Seed"

During 2004 I spent almost every Sunday afternoon with six men. We would get together for about two hours each week for Bible discussion, prayer, and accountability. We called this an Impact group and worked through four discipleship courses that were all based on having the same type of impact that Christ had. At the end of the yearlong commitment, we all made another commitment. Dwight, Dave, Tom, Scott, Jason, Mark, and I all agreed to recruit and lead our own Impact groups during 2005.

As I write this chapter, I have in front of me a list of the men who are going through the Impact course with one of the six guys in my original Sunday afternoon group. There are twenty-five names on the page. I think that is really cool! I think it will be even cooler when many of those twenty-five start their own groups in 2006. In a few years I won't have a piece of paper big enough to list all the names. In fact, I won't even know all the guys who are being influenced.

At this point in the disciple-making process, I can count all the people who are involved. At some point, counting the number of people involved in the process will be impossible. That is the beauty of multiplication. As someone has said, "Anyone can count the seeds in an apple, but no one can count the apples in a seed." What a powerful statement. Today, "I can count twenty-five seeds in the apple, but I cannot begin to count the apples in the seed."

In Colossians 1:6 Paul writes, *"...All over the world this gospel is bearing fruit and growing, just as it has been doing among you since the day you heard it and understood God's grace in all its truth."* Paul tells us two important truths in that verse.

First, Paul's words tell us there must have been many apples in a few seeds. Think about this for a moment. Jesus poured His life into twelve seeds. He shared life with them, taught them, and commissioned them to do the same with others. Now, Paul indicates that in a relatively short number of years after Christ's life, those few seeds were bearing fruit and growing all over the world. That gives you chill bumps, doesn't it?

The second thing I see in Paul's statement is that seeds are made to produce fruit. In other words, multiplying disciples is a natural response to hearing and understanding God's grace! A seed was never created for the purpose of simply remaining a seed. I hate to say it, but I know so many Christians who have settled for living as a lifelong seed. Please don't fall into that trap. Seeds that stay seeds have missed the very purpose for which they were created. The purpose of life is not to become a better seed. The purpose of life is to be a seed that eventually bears fruit. God made you a disciple to make more disciples!

You probably already see this coming, but you do know what must happen for a seed to bear fruit don't you? It must first die. Ouch! This all sounded pretty good up until now. Who on earth wants to die?

Dying to self is the key to becoming a reproducing disciple. Giving up two hours on Sunday afternoons for a year, being committed to preparing a lesson each week, allowing someone to hold you accountable, and consistently praying for a few fellow disciples is an act of self sacrifice. Honestly, this level of sacrifice pales in comparison to dying on a cross, but only a few people I know are even willing to go this far.

So, what about you? Are you happy just being a seed? Have you gotten comfortable staying right in the middle of a plump, juicy piece of fruit? Are you willing to be planted? Are you willing to die so that others might live?

I encourage you to find a few individuals into whom you can pour your life. Just like Jesus, choose a few seeds and give them all you have. Teach them how to be a disciple of Christ then send them out to do the same with others. Spend a year with these seeds and watch what God does as the seeds produce more apples. You might even realize that is why you were created.

Day Sixteen:
"The Unlikely Seed"

I remember this like it was yesterday. I was serving as a student pastor in a new church when one Sunday night the congregation had a watermelon eating fellowship following the evening service. I ate my piece of watermelon with a group of teenagers who were having the best time spitting seeds at each other. We were seed spitting right next to a place where the ground had recently been bulldozed for a construction project. Seeds were going everywhere.

A very funny thing happened a few months later. As I walked alongside the new building, I noticed a vine growing in the same area where the seed spitting had taken place. That's right, a watermelon vine! Imagine that. A wayward seed had just happened to find its way into the fresh soil, soaked up enough water, and germinated. In a matter of weeks we had a watermelon growing right beside the church. I guess you could say this church was truly bearing fruit.

The watermelon never got very big and it wasn't very sweet, but it did make for an awesome children's sermon. I must admit it not only made a good children's sermon, but it also spoke to me.

God used a wayward watermelon seed to teach me the importance of bearing fruit. In a very unlikely way, God revealed to me that He has placed within each of us a natural desire to reproduce more disciples. Think about it. How did a seed with no nurturing produce a watermelon? It wasn't correctly planted. The ground wasn't fertile. No one watered or weeded the vine as it grew. No one even knew the plant was there until the fruit was produced.

This surprise watermelon vine reminds me that God has created us to multiply the life of Christ in others. Multiplication is part of our discipleship DNA. We should be reproducing disciples even if we are never trained or equipped to do so. Multiplying other disciples is what we are created for. The Creator is honored when the creation does what the Creator designed it to do. In John 15:8 Jesus says, *"This is to My Father's glory, that you bear much fruit, showing yourselves to be My disciples."*

I know a guy who was a wayward seed. He stumbled across the idea of multiplying disciples. No one ever instructed him or equipped him with an understanding of multiplying disciples. He never took a course on making disciples. He did not grow up in a church where multiplying disciples was taught or encouraged. He never had a mentor who showed him the disciple-making ropes. He never even had anyone disciple him.

This fellow stumbled on disciple making when he invited a few teenagers to meet with him each week in his parent's basement for Bible study, prayer, and accountability. The basement experience was so rich that he did it again while working as a youth pastor in seminary. He invested in a small group of teenage men through weekly meetings, weekend witnessing efforts, and simply hanging out together. While serving as a youth pastor, he even designed a discipleship course for all the students in his youth ministry.

In time, this young man accepted a position as a pastor in a new church. Without any instruction or counsel, he decided to lead this church to do what he had done as a youth pastor. He led them to begin to be a movement of multiplying disciples. The process is still developing. One would be hard pressed to define this church as a multiplying movement at this point. It is, however, the closest thing I have ever seen to being a church that is multiplying disciples. I do know that many of the people in this church are bearing fruit, and that gives the Father glory.

I will continue to be a seed that seeks to bear fruit for the Father's glory. That is why He created me. I am a seed that was created to reproduce fruit for the Father. God has taken this wayward seed and given me a vision that I can never shake—the vision of a multiplied life!

So, what about you? Are you fruitful or barren? Are you planting in the lives of others? Are you committed to a life of disciple making? Have you grasped God's vision of a reproduced life? Are you bringing the Father glory by bearing fruit for Him?

Day Seventeen:
"The Basement Bunch"

I had absolutely no clue what I was doing. My girlfriend invited me to speak at a youth retreat for a church where she was the student director. The retreat was a huge success, and I decided to invite a few of the guys to meet with me each week in the basement of my parents' house.

We met on Thursday nights for an hour or two, and the first thing we did was ask each other how our week had gone. I asked each guy how his walk with God was going, and where he might be having a victory or a struggle. The discussion was great. We truly opened up and gave each other an inside look at our spiritual development.

Once we had shared our experiences of the past week, we opened up God's Word for a time of study. We had no formal approach to our study time; we simply took a book of the Bible and talked about it in a verse-by-verse fashion. We had a great time wrestling with the truths of Scripture and facing questions we had no answers for until the next week. The hunger for learning certainly fueled our fire.

The "Basement Bunch" broke up after a year or so, and I keep in regular contact with only one of the five guys. Two of these young men are now pastors in local churches, and another, Keith, is leading a small discipleship group in a new church plant. Keith is passing the baton. He is doing exactly what Psalm 78:4 says, *"...tell the next generation..."*

Twenty years after the basement gathering, I was teaching a seminary class where I met Mike, a student in the class. Mike and I hit it off right away. He was a youth pastor passionate for disciple making. As a result of our relationship, Mike took some discipleship curriculum that I had developed to use in his youth ministry. When he shared the curriculum with his leadership team, one of the men asked, "Where is this Ken Adams from?"

That man's name was Keith. Yeah, Keith from the Basement Bunch twenty years before. Isn't it amazing how God works?

Several months after completing the seminary class, Mike became a church planter. Our church helped him launch a new congregation which is very committed to being a disciple-making church. Guess who is helping Mike lead the disciple-making charge. You guessed it—Keith.

Like ripples in a pond, disciple making makes a lasting impact. You never know how God is going to use the investments you make in people. Who would have ever thought that meeting with a group of sixteen-year-old kids in my parents' basement would still be impacting people's lives more than twenty years down the road?

Where are you investing your life these days? Are you strategically meeting with a few individuals to help them walk as Jesus walked? Are you building disciples?

I want to encourage you to make an investment in other people. Make time in your life for teaching others how to be a disciple and how to build more disciples. Start a basement gathering. You never know where the ripples will go. God will take care of the ripples if you will just be the rock.

Day Eighteen:
"Germs and Disciple Making"

I had a funny thing happen to me just the other day. I was talking to some fellow pastors about a television special I had recently watched on the subject of "germs." I was amazed to discover that one of the places we are most likely to catch life-threatening germs is inside hospitals. Death from hospital germs is actually the fourth leading cause of death in the United States. Isn't that unbelievable?

As I was sharing this new-found information with my buddies, one of the guys in the group said that early in his ministry, his pastor had taught him to always wash his hands after making a hospital visit. I started to laugh because I had worked for this same pastor prior to my buddy working for him, and he had taught me the exact same habit. My buddy and I joked about how many hand-washing disciples this pastor has made over the years then we laughed at how many people we had passed the same habit on to ourselves.

If this keeps going, one day we may have pastors in "all nations" washing away the germs after making hospital visits. The mandate could be, *"Go into all nations and make hand-washing pastors by baptizing them, and teaching them how to wash their hands."* I think we might be on to something here!

Think how big this hand-washing movement could become. We could start schools on pastoral hand washing and write books on hand-washing techniques. We could hold seminars on the most contemporary methods of washing hands. I'm starting to get very excited! This thing could get so big we could talk about hand washing until Jesus comes back.

Amazing, isn't it? Look how easy it is to pass on a simple habit such as washing your hands when leaving a hospital, and how difficult it is to impart the life of Christ to others. Isn't it unbelievable how many pastors go about learning how to do the Great Commission, yet never do it? I am afraid we have institutionalized the Great Commission to the point that we talk about it much more than we actually do it. At best, we only do one or two parts of it. We "go" and "baptize," but do we teach people to multiply?

The real question we need to be asking ourselves is, "Are we teaching others to live the life Jesus lived?"

Disciple making is all about existing to help people come to faith, grow, and make more disciples of Christ. We must resist the temptation to make it more complicated than that.

I am not against seminaries. I graduated from a very good one. I am not against books on the Christian life, and I have a library full of them. I am not against church seminars. I teach one myself. I am only concerned that the possibility exists for us to lose sight of the simple process of investing the life of Christ in others.

When it is all said and done, we need to be able to look back and know that we have poured the life of Christ into a few people, and in turn, they have done the same with others. We can't be responsible for the long-term results. We simply need to be faithful in imparting the life of Christ to others.

As I think back on it, I don't even remember the first time I followed my pastor into the hospital restroom to wash up. It was just a natural thing for him, and he only told me one time why he did it. I was immediately convinced this was a practice I wanted to continue the rest of my life. I believed in it so much I have taught several others to do the same. When I started washing my hands after a hospital visit, I didn't even know hospital germs were the fourth leading cause of death! If someone had not taught me the importance of washing away hospital germs, I could have been dead years ago. I suppose I ought to tell as many pastors as I can about hand washing after hospital visits. I guess now you're glad you bought this book!

Day Nineteen:
"Striped Shirts and Spiked Hair"

I get a real kick out of going to pastors' conferences. I am a people watcher, and watching pastors really is a hoot. Pastors, like everyone else, get caught up in what is hot, and what is not. The perfect example these days is the way pastors dress. If you go to a gathering of pastors today, you will find 70-80% of the male pastors wearing long sleeve striped shirts, blue jeans, sandals, and have their hair gelled and spiked. Just a few years ago, you would have attended the same event to find 70-80% of the male pastors wearing Dockers-style pants and golf shirts and hair with not a drop of gel in it.

Obviously, multiplication does happen among pastors. We seem to be very good at spreading whatever is the latest and greatest. We may be great at multiplying a "look," but how well are we doing at multiplying a "life"? As I understand it, everyone who has faith in Jesus will be doing what He did—living like He lived! In John 14:12 Jesus said, *"I tell you the truth, anyone who has faith in Me will do what I have been doing. He will do even greater things than these, because I am going to the Father."*

I think one of the first steps in multiplication is simply to have an understanding of what is to be multiplied. We all know Jesus has commissioned us to multiply disciples. The problem starts when we attempt to define what a disciple looks like. If you asked five pastors to define a disciple, you would get five different answers. How could that possibly be what Jesus had in mind when He told us to make disciples?

Do you think the original disciples sat around after Jesus had ascended back to heaven and debated which disciple would be the model? Would they make disciples who looked like Peter, James, or John? No way! All the disciples knew that the model for making more disciples was Jesus. Their commission was to multiply disciples who had the character and conduct of Jesus Christ.

Multiplying disciples who look like the model does not mean you have to be a perfect disciple. If we wait until we are perfect to multiply disciples, there won't be much multiplying taking place. Multiplying disciples simply means pointing people to the Master. Our goal as disciple makers is to point people to Jesus. All disciples of Jesus should have His mission, follow His model, and use His methodology. All disciples of Jesus should be a part of His movement. Making a disciple is not rocket science. Making disciples means doing what Jesus did and helping others do the same. This may not be the latest and greatest concept in the Christian marketplace, but it is the timeless and changeless pattern for how every Christ follower ought to live. We all should live like Jesus lived.

If Jesus were around today, He might wear a striped shirt, blue jeans and have His hair spiked. I really don't know and don't think it really matters. I do think Jesus would be living in authentic community, demonstrating godly character, growing deeper in His time with the Father, reaching the lost, and teaching the saved. Bottom line, I think Jesus would care a lot more about what a man looks like on the inside rather than on the outside.

So, how about you? What are you multiplying these days? Are you jumping on the bandwagon of the latest Christian craze, or are you staying focused on the Master and intentionally pointing others to Him? Wear all the hair gel you want. Just be sure people find Jesus under all that gel!

Day Twenty:
"Go Hungry"

Whom do you take to the next level? Whom do you invest in for the long haul? When you decide to make the commitment to make disciples, how do you select the right person?

I have a weight room in the basement of my house. Now don't misunderstand. This is not your typical basement weight room set up. I'm not talking about a set of plastic weights and a jump rope in the corner of the playroom. Over the years, I have collected hundreds of pounds of free weights and dumbbells. I have four fitness-center weight machines and a number of benches taking up one third of the space in my basement. You can do some serious damage in this basement weight room!

Through the years, I have had a number of individuals "commit" to working out with me. Some of those commitments have lasted a week. A few have lasted a month or two, but one has lasted over five years!

Alan and I have been working out together two to three days a week for over five years. His commitment has obviously been different from that of the other individuals who have wanted to work out with me. Alan has gone the distance. His hunger for working out has placed him in a whole different classification. Alan and I have actually written several names of people who have quit working out with us on the wall of the basement with the letters "R.I.P." beside their names. These individuals were just not that hungry.

When I think about the way Jesus selected His disciples, I think of the word "hungry." I think Jesus invested in His disciples because they demonstrated a serious commitment to following Him. In John 1:39 the Bible says, *"...So they went and saw where He was staying, and spent that day with Him."* In John 1:43 the Bible says, *"The next day [they] decided to leave for Galilee."* Jesus was looking for individuals who were willing to go beyond the crowd. He looked for people who showed commitment and were hungry for more.

In years of leading small discipleship groups, I have seen a number of men who were hungry to grow. They were willing to pay the price and go the distance. I have also seen my share of one-week wonders. There will always be those who buy the book, show up for the first meeting, but are never to be seen again. Moving from the crowd to the committed was just too hard for them. There will, however, always be a handful of Alans who go the distance and show up every time you meet, ready to learn. These are the hungry! These are the people who start in the crowd and end up as the called.

I do not know where you are in your journey of building disciples, but let me suggest two things. First, be hungry! Stay hungry for a spiritual workout. Keep your heart soft and pliable. Do not allow your desire for spiritual growth to wane. Secondly, look for hungry people! Pour your life into people who want more. Invest in individuals who demonstrate commitment, rather than just talk about it. Look for the person who has already chosen to go to Galilee.

Whom do you take to the next level? Whom do you invest in for the long haul? When you decide to make the commitment to make disciples, how do you select the right person?

In the spiritual weight room of life, there are those who are hungry and those who talk about being hungry. Be a hungry disciple and look for others who are also hungry. These people are the ones in whom you want to invest.

Day Twenty-One:
"One Hungry Dude"

As I write today, I am in the fifth week of a new discipleship group. I meet every week with seven men for what is called an Impact Basics group. We are in a twelve-week course called <u>Know That You Know</u>, a study on ten of the basic doctrines of the Christian faith. Studying basic doctrine is a foundational step for becoming a mature disciple of Jesus.

Jeff, a member of our group, is a perfect example of being hungry. Three or four months before I started this new group, Jeff approached me after a weekend worship service asking me what I recommended for deeper spiritual growth. I told him that his first step would be to join a small fellowship group designed for Bible discussion, prayer, caring, and fellowship. Once he joined a fellowship group, I suggested he might then attend a small men's discipleship group. Both of these groups would be keys to having the proper environment in his life for spiritual growth.

I really didn't expect to hear any more from Jeff; however, within a couple weeks, he had found a small fellowship group to attend and was ready to join a men's discipleship group. I told him to check back with me in a few weeks, and I'd let him know when the group would start. I figured Jeff would settle into his fellowship group, and I would not hear from him again. It was not too long before he once again approached me after a church service to inquire about the start-up of our men's group. I asked him to keep in touch with me and told him I planned to begin the group in a month or so. This time I had little doubt that Jeff would once again be calling. Like clockwork, he sent me an e-mail and telephoned my assistant about three weeks after our last conversation.

Even though I had talked to Jeff a number of times following church services, I did not really know him very well. The one thing I did know about Jeff was that he was one spiritually hungry dude. Very rarely does a person keep asking to be a part of a spiritual growth environment the way he did. Jeff's persistence made my decision to include him in my group a no-brainer. His attitude made me think about what Jesus said in Matthew 16:24 which says, *"If anyone would come after Me, he must deny himself and take up his cross and follow Me."* How interesting that Jesus is talking to His followers in this verse, not seekers. Jesus challenged those who were hungry and in the Christ crowd to take a deeper step with Him and raise their level of commitment.

Jesus' call to commitment reminds me of something I read from Art Turbock. He said, *"There is a difference between interest and commitment. When you are interested in doing something, you only do it when circumstances permit. When you are committed to something, you accept no excuses, only results."* Jesus did not choose the "interested" in whom to invest His life; He invested in the "committed"!

Are you building disciples because your circumstances permit it, or are you building disciples because you know God has commissioned us to do so? Being interested will not make you a multiplier but being committed will.

Do you know someone who is hungry? Do you have a Jeff in your life? Why not have some spiritual conversations with people before you start investing your life in them? Take time to test the waters before you dive into a disciple-making relationship. Checking a person's spiritual temperature is important before you commit to a significant investment of your life.

I cannot tell you where Jeff will be two years from now. I do not know if he'll be investing in a handful of disciples or not. I do know that as long as he is hungry, I will be willing to invest in him until he is equipped to make disciples. I'm excited to see how the rest of Jeff's story plays out.

Jesus did not know what His disciples would do either. Would they obey His command to make disciples, or reject it? You know the rest of their story. Jesus must have found some hungry dudes, and they must have passed on what He gave them to another bunch of hungry folks. Hungry disciples make hungry disciples!

Day Twenty-Two:
"She Gets It"

Only one reference in Scripture refers to Jesus being full of joy. In Luke 10:21 the Bible says, *"At that time Jesus, full of joy through the Holy Spirit, said, 'I praise you, Father, Lord of heaven and earth, because You have hidden these things from the wise and learned, and revealed them to little children. Yes, Father, for this was Your good pleasure.'"* I believe Jesus is described as being "full of joy" because He knows His disciples get it. In Luke chapter 10, Jesus is listening to the report of the seventy-two after they had returned from preaching in other towns. He had sent them out, and they came back with a better understanding of the mission. They got it!

Nothing brings a disciple maker more joy than to see the person in whom he invested turn around and invest in someone else. When the individual you have poured your life into begins to multiply into the lives of others, you know they "get it." The light has come on. The elevator has reached the top floor. The cake is baked.

I recently received a note from Patty, a woman in our church who gets it. Look at part of what she wrote to me.

"Well here I am in <u>Impact One</u> again for the fourth, or fifth, or whatever time. Discipleship, before coming to this church, was basically a course you took someone through and hoped she gleaned something from it. Now I have the complete picture and conviction of what discipleship is meant to be. The best use of my time, or anyone else's time, is impacting someone else for Jesus."

Patty gets it! She is a dear woman who is a very solid Bible teacher and has served in ministry and leadership for many years. Patty is a "fully trained" Christ follower who has come to understand that investing her life in making disciples is the one thing that will outlast her lifetime. Patty has moved from programs to a disciple-making process, from information overload to a balance of information and application, and from consumerism to disciple making. She has demonstrated a willingness to keep walking people through a disciple-making process even when she has done it many times over. Patty gets it. She has realized it is not about, "What is in it for me?"

I hate to say it, but very few people I have discipled ever get it. You spend months investing in people so they will invest in others, and all they want is more Bible study. You spend months equipping others to reproduce, and then they say they are not ready to lead someone else. Or on the other hand, they end up being busy about another church program. I wish the world had more people like Patty.

When the person you disciple begins to disciple someone else, it brings you joy. That is the disciple maker's dream come true. When reproduction happens, you know there is the chance a lineage has begun that might continue until Jesus comes back. There is no greater joy than knowing you have invested your life in a way that will outlast the brief time you will have here on earth.

How would Jesus have felt if His disciples had said, "Lord, we want more Bible study"? What would Jesus have done if His disciples had said, "Lord, we need to stay together for more fellowship"? Imagine how Jesus would have felt if His disciples had said, "Jesus, we are too busy to make disciples." If any of the above had happened to Jesus, I think He would have been full of sadness instead of full of joy.

So, what about you? Are you giving joy to the person who discipled you? When you bring joy to the person who discipled you, you bring joy to God. Do you get it?

Day Twenty-Three:
"One Bad Apple"

When I was a child, there was a popular song that had the lyrics, *"One bad apple don't spoil the whole bunch girl. Oh give it one more try before you give up on love."* Well, I did give it one more try. Rejection did not stop me from eventually finding love for a lifetime. With great determination and much persistence, I finally found a woman who had enough sympathy to take me in and spend the rest of her life with me.

Disciple making is another venture that requires great determination and persistence. You can spend major amounts of time investing in potential disciple makers and actually only have one in the bunch who reproduces another disciple of Christ. That one disciple is worth it! Even if only one person grasps Christ's commission for making disciples, then your time has been well spent. That one person could eventually impact thousands of people for Christ through multiplication.

Even Jesus experienced rejection from some of those in whom He invested His life. In John 6:66 the Bible says, *"From this time many of His disciples turned back and no longer followed Him."* Did you catch the reference for that verse? I find it interesting that the verse describing a rejection of Christ is 6:66!

Can you imagine how Jesus must have felt when "many" of His disciples rejected Him? Do you think Jesus was discouraged or wondered if making disciples was worth it? Do you think He felt like giving up on investing in others?

I believe Jesus felt the same emotions we feel. I believe He was hurt by those who walked away and felt the same pain we do when somebody rejects us. I wonder if Jesus maybe even debated with the Father about using a method other than "disciples" to reach the world.

As Paul Harvey would say, we know "the rest of the story." We know that Jesus did not give up on the Father's disciple-making strategy. We know that He persisted in His investment in committed followers. We know that He pressed past the pain of rejection and poured His life into a faithful few. We know that He did not let a few bad apples spoil the plan to reach "all nations."

I think anyone who is serious about making disciples will experience the very same things Jesus experienced. I know I have. In over twenty-five years of disciple making, I have a list of men who became bad apples. One example is a man in whom I invested several years of my life. When the disobedience in his life was challenged, he decided to turn back and follow no more. He left me a voice mail filled with profanity and demanded that I "stay out of his life and out of his way." His ex-wife and kids are still paying the price for his sin.

One bad apple has not spoiled the whole bunch of disciples in whom I have invested. I can tell you that people like Keith, Rodney, Randy, Alan, Tim, Sandy, Rebecca, Kevin, Mike, Tom, Nick, John, Ken, Mark, Bob, Dwight, Scott, and dozens of others have made all my efforts worthwhile. These are just names to you, but to some people, these are the folks who have given them a vision for walking as Jesus walked!

How strong is your vision for building disciples? Is it strong enough to handle rejection? Is it resilient enough to handle those who turn away and choose to no longer follow? Do you press on in the disciple-making process even when it is no longer the hot thing to do? Is disciple making a fad for you, or is it a conviction that burns red-hot in your being?

Don't let one or more bad apples spoil a lifetime commitment to making disciples of Jesus Christ. If you stay the course, God will use your efforts to fill a bushel basket full of fruit.

Day Twenty-Four:
"Your Most Important Disciple"

I had been making disciples of men for several decades before I finally discovered who my most important disciples are. It took awhile, but God finally helped me realize my most important disciples are my own children.

It all started when my oldest son, Caleb, was ten years old. I had a heavy burden on my heart to invest more time in his spiritual development. I truly wanted to teach him how to walk with God, but I just didn't seem to have the time.

I still remember very vividly standing on a football field having a conversation with God about this very issue. I was coaching Caleb's football team when, during one of our three, two-hour, weekly practices, God spoke to my heart. As I stood there watching the team do exercises, I could sense God saying, *"You know, Ken Adams, you say you don't have time to disciple your son, but you have time to spend six to eight hours a week in football. Your problem is not having enough time. Your problem is how you are spending it."*

If I remember correctly, this is when a light shone from heaven, and I got down on my knees as an organ started playing, "Just As I Am." I confessed my sin right there on that ball field and told God I would make no more excuses. I went home from football practice that August evening with a commitment to invest in my son's spiritual development.

Looking for a discipleship tool for a father and son was more of a challenge than I realized. As I combed the shelves of Christian bookstores, I finally concluded that such a tool did not exist. That conclusion left me with one option: I needed to develop one. Over the next several weeks, I began writing a father/son discipleship tool that taught the importance of being a disciple of Christ.

During the writing of this book, I also did a little research and development. I invited three other fathers and sons to join Caleb and me for a discipleship group meeting once a week to share life, discuss our lessons, pray, and hold each other accountable for certain things.

The results of our months together were amazing. I had more intentional spiritual time with my son than I had ever known. Our time working on our lessons and doing ministry projects together was excellent. In addition, our "hang" time together was great. The best part of it all, however, was the conversations we had driving home from our weekly group time. In those fifteen minutes, we talked about things we might never have talked about any other time.

The months I spent with Caleb in <u>Impact Partners</u> were the closest I think I have ever come to applying Deuteronomy 6:6-9: *"These commandments that I give you today are to be upon your hearts. Impress them on your children. Talk about them when you sit at home and when you walk along the road, when you lie down and when you get up. Tie them as symbols on your hands and bind them on your foreheads. Write them on the doorframes of your homes and on your gates."*

As I am writing this book to inspire and motivate people to build more disciples, I cannot leave out this chapter on realizing who your most important disciples are. I would hate to see mothers or fathers become mega-multipliers yet forget to disciple their own children!

Day Twenty-Five:
"Impress Them On Your Children"

If you have children, you know full well that I can't say something about one child and leave out the others. That is why I need to take another chapter to tell you about the time my wife led my daughter, Kelsi, through a mother/daughter discipleship group, and I led my youngest son, Connor, through a father/son discipleship group. Kelsi and my wife, Val, met with several other moms and daughters for a young girls' edition of Impact Partners. In the meantime, I led a group with Connor and three other men and their boys.

The group Connor and I were a part of with the other fathers and sons was incredible. We met every Saturday morning to discuss our weekly lesson, pray, and share what God was doing in our lives. Words cannot describe what it feels like to hear your own offspring share a spiritual insight from Scripture or pray a heartfelt petition to God.

I think the irony of the whole concept is that the kids usually end up pushing the adults during the course. Deuteronomy 6:7 tells us to, *"Impress them [God's commandments] on our children."* When your child is pushing you to do the Bible lesson and memorize your verse before the group meeting, I am not sure who impresses whom. Either way, the process of making disciples is being accomplished.

Watching all three of my children go through a discipleship course with a parent has left me with the conviction that every child needs such an experience. Investing the life of Christ into your own children is a parent's number one responsibility. It is not the church's job to disciple your child. Parents are personally responsible for the spiritual well being of their children. Looking back at the investment I made in my kids through discipleship has led me to several important conclusions.

Hands-on Bible study is invaluable for you and your child. As I worked through the lessons with my boys, I was able to teach them the commandments of the Lord. Searching the Scriptures together could never be replaced by a Sunday school class or children's church service.

Small group discussions help to apply the truths of Scripture. I can't describe the many ways a Scripture we had studied in our lessons took on a whole new meaning when it was discussed in the context of the small group. One story or insight from a father or son brought the text alive and made an indelible impression.

Accountability is a great motivator. One of the things that helped me make an investment in my children was the accountability we shared with other fathers and sons. I can safely say that I would not have been as intentional about discipling my children if I had not asked other fathers and sons to do this with me. There is incredible power in accountability.

Fellowship is a great way to practice the "one anothers." The Bible is filled with expressions of how we are to treat each other in the body of Christ. The weekly share times I experienced with other fathers and sons gave us a great outlet for encouraging and supporting one another.

Ministry is an exciting challenge. In all of the months of father/son discipleship, we did many different kinds of ministry projects. I still remember the Saturday morning when four father-and-son teams passed out free sodas in front of a local store. Nothing is more exciting than doing ministry alongside your child with other fathers and sons.

Well, I hope you've gotten the point by now. Make disciples, but start with your own family! Build disciples at home before you go anywhere else. If you disciple your children well, they will multiply the life of Christ in others. Multiplying disciples of Jesus Christ is the reason you exist to begin with.

Day Twenty-Six:
"Making Time, Making Disciples"

I'm always amazed at how many times I hear the statement, "I wish I could make disciples, but I just don't have the time." I don't usually say it, but I always think it...baloney! We all know that having enough time is never our problem, but managing our time is the problem. God has given each of us the exact same amount of time. We all have 168 hours in a week to be used for God's glory.

I have always been big on staying in shape physically. In fact, the older I get, the rounder my shape is becoming! Nevertheless, over the years I have always made time for cardio and weight training. When I was in college, I would get up at 5:30 and go for a run to start the day. Then my schedule changed, and I began working out during my lunch break.

When I began a career, I changed my workout time to the late afternoons following my workday. I even worked out late at night for a few years. I guess over the past thirty years, I have worked out at almost every hour of the day. I have changed my workout time often, but I have always made time for working out.

The point I am trying to make is that we make time for the things that are important to us. This was certainly the case with Jesus. Check out what the Scriptures say about the time Jesus planned for disciple making:

Mark 3:7 — *"Jesus withdrew with His disciples to the lake, and a large crowd from Galilee followed."*

Mark 4:34 — *"...But when He was alone with His own disciples, He explained everything."*

Mark 6:30 — *"The apostles gathered around Jesus and reported to Him all they had done and taught."*

Mark 14:32 — *"They went to a place called Gethsemane, and Jesus said to His disciples, 'Sit here while I pray.'"*

These verses are only a sampling of the many references concerning the time Jesus spent with His disciples. If you get anything from these references, get this. If Jesus made time in His busy schedule to invest in a handful of disciples, how can we be too busy to do the same?

I want you to know that if you are too busy to make disciples of Christ, you are just too busy! You have been given the amount of time God wants you to have. He expects you to manage it for His purposes, not your own.

Over the years, I have had to change the meeting times with the men in whom I was investing my life. I have had discipleship groups that met at 5:30 in the morning and others that met during lunch. I have met with a group of men on Saturday mornings and another on Tuesday nights. I have even met with a group of men on Sunday afternoon. Preaching on Sunday mornings has never made Sunday afternoon a convenient time, but convenience is not my goal. Honoring God by making disciples of Jesus Christ is my goal.

You have the time to lead a small group of men or women in becoming more like Jesus Christ. The issue is not that you don't have the time. The issue is managing your time according to God's agenda rather than your own.

So, what about it? Whose agenda are you following? Are you going to honor God by making time to make disciples?

Day Twenty-Seven:
"Disciples, Not Just Decisions"

I have coached each of my kids in the Little League sports of baseball, basketball, and football. In each of these sports I have always stressed the fact that it does not matter whether you win or lose, but how you play the game. That philosophy works well at the Little League level, but it is a hard argument to make at the higher levels of athletic competition. People really want to win!

I remember a conversation at a baseball game with a man who made the statement, "If winning didn't matter, they wouldn't keep score." How you play the game is important, but winning at all costs is not the answer. However, we do compete in the athletic arena in order to win. College basketball teams do not celebrate having the most rebounds if they lose the NCAA Tournament. Major League baseball teams do not commemorate having the most stolen bases if they lose the World Series. National League football teams do not congratulate each other on having the fewest penalties if they lose the Super Bowl.

Have you ever noticed that churches keep score? Yes, they really do. In fact, I grew up in a church that had a scoreboard hanging right behind the piano in the sanctuary. The little wooden board had a place to record worship attendance, Sunday school attendance, weekly offering, and the number of visitors. Obviously, keeping the score was important in this church. Too bad we kept the wrong score!

I know attendance and offering are important numbers, and I know why church leaders post them for the members to see. I know certain numbers are indicators of health and fruitfulness. I also know that the only number that matters on God's scoreboard is how many disciples we've made. This is why Luke wrote in Acts 6:7, *"So the Word of God spread. The number of disciples in Jerusalem increased rapidly, and a large number of priests became obedient to the faith."* Luke did not write, *"The offering grew, and we entered into a huge building project."* Nothing is wrong with increasing the offering or building new facilities if offerings and buildings are the product of more disciples.

Let me try to clarify my argument. I believe the reason we exist is to have a relationship with God and to help others have the same; in a nutshell—to be a disciple of Christ and to build more disciples of Christ.

All the numbers we keep must come back to the main goal—being and building disciples. My experience tells me that very few Christians and churches are measuring the most important number. The majority of Christians and churches I have known are measuring *decisions* made for Christ, more than *disciples* made for Christ. We reach out to people, help them come to faith in Christ, and then the rest is up to them. Our attitude seems to be, "If they stick, great, and if they don't, oh well."

In light of Christ's commission to *"make disciples of all nations, baptizing them...and teaching them to obey all that He commanded,"* we need to reach out to people, and help them grow to the place where they are doing the same with others. That is making disciples. That is a multiplying movement of disciple makers!

Okay, look at your personal scoreboard. Who is winning? Better yet, what are you measuring? Are you measuring decisions, or are you measuring disciples? Yes, reach out to as many people as possible who need Christ. Yes, lead them to a point of baptism and church membership. Yes, help them find a place to serve in the church. No, do not drop them at this point in the process. Yes, train them and teach them how to make more disciples. Yes, watch over them until they become a proven disciple maker. Now, put a one on the scoreboard and celebrate!

Day Twenty-Eight:
"Excuses"

Don't you just hate listening to someone who is constantly giving excuses? You know what I mean … one who has an excuse for things not done or why things did not turn out the way they should.

I'll admit it. I've suffered from excuse abuse myself at times. Over the years, I have made all kinds of excuses for why I don't exercise, why I don't eat right, and why I don't finish projects around the house. I could go on and on about the thousands of ways I've made excuses for not doing what I knew needed to be done.

Although He is much more understanding and patient than I am, I think even God has a hard time handling excuse abuse. I guess the spiritual way to say it is that it *"grieves God's Spirit"* (Ephesians 4:30). I think the truth is, "it ticks God off"! I do know that when you read stories of the children of Israel and Moses, half the time God was talking Moses out of destroying the people, and the other half of the time Moses was talking God out of destroying them.

Look at the story of the talents in Matthew 25:14-30. Jesus tells a parable about three men who were given a certain amount of money then held accountable for what they had done with it. Two of the three men multiplied their money. One man buried his money and brought back the same amount he had been given. Listen to the excuse he gave to his master in verse 25, *"So I was afraid and went out and hid your talent in the ground."* In the next verse, the master refers to this servant as *"wicked and lazy."* Wow, Jesus did not like excuses any more than we do. In verse 30 the master says, *"And throw that worthless servant outside, into the darkness, where there will be weeping and gnashing of teeth."*

Through the years, I have read this parable and thought I needed to do a better job of investing my money or abilities, etc. Today, I read this parable and think about the importance of multiplying my life for Christ. I don't want to come to the end of my days and have nothing but excuses for God about why I did not build more disciples. I don't want to be too busy, too afraid, too stubborn, or for my life to be so cluttered that I never have time to make disciples. I don't want to let anything stop me from hearing my Master say, *"Well done, good and faithful servant"* (Matthew 25:21 and 23)!

Everyone I know is busy these days. I just hope you are busy about the right things. Let me encourage you to avoid any excuse that keeps you from being a disciple maker or making more disciple makers. When you come to the end of your days, make sure you have multiplied your life for Christ! No more excuse abuse.

Day Twenty-Nine:
"Ripples"

Just about everyone at some time has stood on the bank of a pond or lake and tossed a rock into the water. Once the rock entered the water, one ripple produced multiple ripples. One rock can create a profound effect on the condition of an entire pond.

A few weeks ago, I felt like a kid standing on the bank of a pond throwing rocks in the water. It was between services at the church where I serve as pastor when I walked into my office and greeted seven men who were meeting for discipleship. Tom and Scott were leading the group. They are two men I had spent an entire year with in a discipleship environment. Since our discipleship group last met, they have been meeting every week with Chris, Rob, Troy, Buck, and Donnie. Tom and Scott are rocks in the pond.

Realizing their group was only a few weeks away from the completion of their course, I asked each of the men what their next step was. All five of them either had already identified potential disciples or were in the process of doing so. Every man in the group was committed to being the next ripple in the pond.

When I walked out of that office, I sensed the same joy I believe Jesus felt when He knew His disciples were committed to making more disciples. I am not naïve enough to think that every one of those men will faithfully multiply other disciples. My experience tells me that even good-hearted disciples do not always pass the baton.

I hope every one of Tom and Scott's disciples will be ripple makers, but if not all of them make ripples that will be okay. Only one rock is needed to make another ripple. If just one of those five men will reproduce what has happened to him, an entire pond could be impacted. In Acts 6:1 the Bible says, *"In those days the number of disciples was increasing..."* That one verse tells me Jesus had at least one ripple maker. At least one of His original disciples passed the baton.

I have no idea how many ripples might result from my investment in Tom and Scott, and that is not for me to worry about. I was obedient to God by pouring my life into them. I threw my rock. Tom and Scott were obedient as well. They threw their rocks. Today five more men have rocks in their hands. My prayer is that each of these men will throw their rocks. I pray that Chris, Buck, Donnie, Rob, and Troy will all be ripple makers of all nations.

Just imagine what would happen if we had a pond's edge full of rock throwers? If we had that, we might actually create a wave. That would be something! Imagine a pond with a wave! Talk about impacting your community for Christ!

I believe Jerusalem was experiencing a wave. The disciples were increasing because they had a whole church full of rock throwers. They had a whole team of ripple makers who were committed to fulfilling the Great Commission.

I am writing this book to inspire a few rock throwers. I know my community needs a wave, and I am betting yours does too. Have you thrown your rock? Do you have a rock in your hand? Let's be ripple-makers for Christ. If we all commit to throwing our rocks, maybe we can start a wave.

Day Thirty:
"I'm Lovin' It"

A very popular fast-food chain has a new slogan out these days. The phrase, "I'm lovin' it" is on hamburger wrappers, cups, and paper bags. An entire ad campaign has been launched around this simple idea.

As I listen to the words in this phrase, I have caught myself wondering exactly who is lovin' it. Is it the consumer who loves the high-fat burgers and fries? Probably! Is it the employees who love serving the consumers? Hardly! Is it the owner who loves his trip to the bank as billions are sold daily? Of the three choices, my guess is the person who makes the trip to the bank is the clear answer.

This fast-food slogan has made me think quite a bit recently about the Great Commission. The similarities are interesting. First, the goal of this food chain is very similar to the mission of the church. This chain wants to sell burgers in every nation of the world. The purpose of the church is to make disciples in all nations. By the way, some might argue that the fast-food chain is making better progress than the church.

Secondly, the product of this food chain is consistent worldwide. Their hamburgers taste the same in Brazil as in the United States. Isn't it amazing how hamburgers can be reproduced with such consistency in a fast-food restaurant, but disciples of Jesus look so different among churches? Maybe we can learn something about making "McFollowers."

Finally, this fast-food chain would want us to have a loveable experience with their food. They want us to think they love us, and that we will also love them. I'm not so sure their motive is pure. "Lovin' it" might sound good, but only if it sells burgers and fries.

Making disciples of Jesus Christ ought to be a "lovin' it" experience. First of all, we ought to make disciples because of love. Loving God and loving people should always lead to making more disciples. Jesus said in Mark 12:30-31, *"Love the Lord your God with all your heart and with all your soul and with all your mind and with all your strength. The second is this: Love your neighbor as yourself."*

Love is to be our motivation for fulfilling the Great Commission. We should be making disciples because we love God and love people. We should not be making disciples because we feel like we "have to" or because we will feel guilty if we don't.

Frankly, I am amazed at the attitudes I have found in some Christians when it comes to the priority of making disciples. I have heard people say things that I know grieve the heart of God. I know one guy who left our church because "he was sick and tired of hearing about the Great Commission." A church member told me we make "too big a deal about making disciples." Countless numbers of people have let their actions, or lack of, speak even louder than their words. I often wonder if they would say those things if Jesus were standing there?

I have consistently invested in a handful of men for the past twenty years; not because I have to, but because I want to. I do believe making disciples is a matter of obedience, but obedience is an expression of love, not guilt.

So, what about you? I hope the fact that you have read this is proof of your love. I hope you are lovin' making disciples. I hope you are lovin' doing the very thing Jesus did. I hope you are lovin' it enough to do it as long as you live!

Day Thirty-One:
"Great Group Meetings"

Christians are known for having plenty of meetings. A large part of the church is about meeting together. Even the book of Hebrews tells us, *"Let us not give up meeting together, as some are in the habit of doing, but let us encourage one another—and all the more as we see the Day approaching"* (Hebrews 10:25). We meet together for a reason; meetings are important.

Building more disciples obviously involves meeting together. Even Jesus made time to meet with the men He called disciples. We see Jesus withdrawing to meet with His disciples repeatedly in the Gospels. Meetings were important to Jesus, and He used them as a strategic environment in the disciple-making process.

Meetings are necessary, but we all know not every meeting is enjoyable. Think about it. Nothing is worse than spending an hour or two in a meeting that bores the life out of everyone. If building disciples requires meeting together, we must understand how to have great group meetings. Entire books are written about creating great group environments, but for now, let's focus on three important ingredients for a discipleship group.

The first ingredient for a great discipleship group meeting is the **Word of God**. If the Bible is not central to your time together, you will not have a very powerful meeting. The goal of every successful disciple-making environment is to bring the truth of God's Word into the context of our lives. When a small group of men or women starts to dig into God's Word together, good things are going to happen! The Bible is the Sword of the Spirit, and it will transform people's lives.

The second ingredient of a great discipleship group meeting is **prayer**. A group that prays together and for each other is a great group. The disciples in the book of Acts devoted themselves to the apostles' teaching and to prayer. A discipleship environment without prayer is like being in a sailboat on a lake with no wind. You may enjoy being in a sailboat with someone, but you would enjoy it even more if the boat was moving. Praying together puts the wind in the sails of spiritual growth.

A final ingredient for a great discipleship group meeting is **accountability**. A group that challenges and encourages each other is always going to be a great group. The interaction between disciples through accountability and encouragement creates an environment for the Bible and prayer to be applied to our lives. No one needs another meeting that does not make one bit of difference in our lives. We need meetings that mean something and cause us to take a serious look at how the things we are learning apply to our lives. The goal of discipleship is not simply the accumulation of more information, but the application of that information. Jesus not only told His disciples to be fishers of men; He helped them do it.

Over the years, I have been in and led countless numbers of discipleship groups. Whenever I have seen a small group of men or women dig into God's Word, pray together, and challenge and encourage one another, good things have happened. These ingredients worked with Jesus' discipleship group, and they will work with yours. Build more disciples and do so with great group meetings.

Day Thirty-Two: "Where's the Beef?"

"Where's the beef?" was a line used in a classic commercial for a popular hamburger chain several years ago. The commercial featured a little hamburger patty in the middle of a huge bun. Obviously, the idea they wanted to communicate was that they sold bigger hamburger patties than any other hamburger place. My experience has shown me that many discipleship groups are like hamburger buns containing little or no meat. Sometimes you come away asking, "Where is the Word?"

As you saw in the previous lesson, one of the essential ingredients to a great group meeting is the Scriptures. The Bible should be the centerpiece for all of your discussion. A group that is not built on the foundation of God's Word is "missing the beef." We do not need groups where we simply share our experiences; rather our experience needs to be examined according to the truth of God. We do not need groups where we just download our feelings; instead, our feelings need to align with the truth of God. We do not need groups where we simply express our opinions. Our opinions mean nothing if they contradict the absolute truth of God. We need discipleship groups where the meat of God's Word intersects where we live.

The disciples in Acts lived in the intersection of life and truth. In Acts 2:42 the Bible says, *"They devoted themselves to the apostles' teaching and to the fellowship, to the breaking of bread and to prayer."* The first century disciples had the beef in their lives. The apostles' teaching they devoted themselves to was the teachings of Christ. The apostles simply passed on to other disciples what they had seen and learned from Christ. The teachings of Jesus were not optional. They were central!

Building disciples through discipleship groups based on the truth of God will require several important priorities. The first priority is **the life and teachings of Christ**. Christ is the curriculum for disciple making and should be the model. Whatever course, workbook, or lesson plan you use to make disciples must reflect the life of Christ.

The second priority is the material should be **easily transferable**. The apostles passed down the teachings of Christ because they were easy to transfer. In order to create a movement of multiplication, you must have content that is easy to pass on. With the life of Christ as the curriculum, it is easy to have a consistent set of lesson plans to follow. Everything you need to make a disciple of Christ can be found in His life and teachings. You cannot go wrong when you teach the life of Christ.

A final priority is **tools that help you focus your teaching efforts**. You can lead a discipleship group without any type of resources or tools since the Bible is really all you will ever need to teach the life of Christ. I have found, however, that a small group resource that is transferable and Christ-based is very helpful. Most people do not have the time to create their own lesson plans for discipleship groups. When you have a disciple-making tool that is very user friendly, your job as a leader will be much easier.

Leading discipleship groups for over twenty-five years has brought me to the place where I saw the need for developing disciple-making resources. Impact Ministries was created to help develop disciple-making tools that teach the life of Christ with transferable principles so leaders can stay focused. I hope you will check out the many resources available at www.impactdiscipleship.com. We will help you provide the beef!

Day Thirty-Three: "Time to Memorize"

One of the best ways to bring truth into the process of building disciples is to make the memorization of Scripture a major objective of the group. Placing a value on the importance of committing God's Word to memory can be difficult, but great things happen when you hide His truth in your heart.

Over the years, I have had some interesting things happen with the Scripture memory part of the group. I have seen some guys repeat verses at machine gun speed, and I have seen others limp to the finish line needing assistance with every word.

I know some guys who completely freeze at the idea of memorizing Scripture while at the same time have dozens of phone numbers committed to memory. I have had groups of disciples where the challenge of memorizing Scripture was like trying to win an arm-wrestling contest. The competitive spirit pushed them to memorize. I had one group that tried to hide sticky notes containing memory verses on the bottom of their shoes and in places within the room so they could smoothly quote the verse.

Without question, the most memorable memory verse experience I have ever had was in a father-and-son discipleship group. In this group, each father and son would quote a memory verse each week. At our final group meeting, a young eleven-year-old named Levi quoted all twenty-six verses from the course! I have not had another disciple do what Levi did in that group. I was very impressed.

The memorization of Scripture is a great spiritual discipline. God's Word stays in your heart and mind. In Psalms 119:11 the psalmist says, *"I have hidden Your Word in my heart that I might not sin against You."* When tempted by Satan in the wilderness, Jesus quoted the Words of Scripture as His defense against Satan's attack.

There is tremendous power in being able to recall the truth of God's Word from memory. When you know what the Scriptures say and where to find specific verses, you have the truth of God on the very tip of your tongue. When you are committed to building disciples, you simply cannot neglect this spiritual discipline.

I would encourage you to make time for the memorization of Scripture in every discipleship group you lead. I start every group meeting with a time for each person to quote the assigned verse they memorized the previous week then we take a few minutes to discuss the meaning of the verse. The discussion helps to solidify the importance of memorizing the verse.

If you are really ambitious, you can quote each verse each week adding the previous week's verse to the present week. Then again, you might not want to set up your group for failure. Memorization comes easier for some than it does for others. Celebrate progress in every member's attempt to hide God's Word in his or her heart.

When the original disciples heard Jesus quote Scripture in the midst of ministry encounters, they knew the importance of committing the truth to memory. I doubt seriously if the disciples ever sat in a circle and challenged each other to recite verses, but I am certain from all of the verses quoted by the apostles in Acts that they made time to memorize!

Day Thirty-Four:
"Fill-in Lives"

One of the biggest mistakes I have seen in discipleship groups is placing too much emphasis on covering the material. I have known discipleship leaders who set out to cover every blank in the book and discuss every point of the outline. Some leaders get so bogged down in the content and go overboard filling in the blanks of the lesson they cannot see the forest for the trees.

I want to suggest a different approach to building disciples—the "fill-in-the-life" method to disciple making is one that balances content with context. The fill-in-the-life leader understands that the goal of the group is transformed lives, not filled-in notebooks!

One time I was meeting with a small group of men when we had a fill-in-the-life experience. I opened the group in typical fashion, and we were making good progress with answering the questions in our discussion guide when one of the men became very vulnerable and began to open up about some serious temptation in his life. He began to share with the group how he had been struggling with a source of temptation that could derail his life. It was at that moment the next blank in the outline did not seem essential. This man's life became the priority of the group. The priority became what he needed to hear from God's Word at that moment.

The openness of this man's struggle became a very teachable moment for the group. We departed from the lesson outline, but we did not depart from the truth. Several guys in the group started sharing Scriptures and encouraging our fellow disciple in the midst of his weakness. This teachable moment took up the majority of our group time. We might not have finished the questions in our book, but we saw the Word of God change a life.

The group experience I just described, and others like it, reminds me of what the writer of Hebrews said in Hebrews 4:12, *"For the Word of God is living and active. Sharper than any double-edged sword, it penetrates even to dividing soul and spirit, joints and marrow; it judges the thoughts and attitudes of the heart."*

When a group of people come together and open the Word of God, something happens. The Holy Spirit uses this kind of environment to intersect our lives with God's truth. The content of the Word pours into the context of a person's life which is the foundation of disciple making. One of the reasons building disciples is so important is because this kind of environment is not possible in a large crowd. Truth can be communicated in a large group, but the application of it is very different in a small group.

In Mark, chapter 4, Jesus teaches a parable in a large crowd beside a lake. In verse 10 of that chapter, Jesus explains the parable in more detail once alone with His twelve disciples. Jesus used the fill-in-the-life approach to building disciples. The objective of disciple making for Jesus was transformed lives—not always filling in the blanks. In fact, Jesus didn't even give His disciples blanks, but He did give them the truth in the context of life.

Being in a small group with people who open the Word of God together is a great experience. Being in a small group where people open their lives to the Word of God is an even better experience!

Day Thirty-Five:
"Tool Box"

I have a friend who always reminds me, "It's all about being smarter than what you are working with." This became obvious to me when I was trying to cut a piece of pipe. Once I had the pipe-cutting tool a friend loaned me, the task of cutting a piece of pipe became quite easy. Having the right tool made a very complicated project a much easier undertaking.

I am constantly meeting people who are passionate about disciple making but don't quite know how to go about it. What seems like a difficult task could be much easier given the right tools. Once you realize that God has called you to make disciples who look like Jesus, you need the right tools to accomplish the job.

When I was seven years old, my grandfather gave me a brand new heavy-duty steel toolbox made for real men who did real work. I still have that toolbox today. I was very excited about having my own toolbox, but I immediately realized there was one problem with this box. It had no tools in it! I would never accomplish much if I did not collect the necessary tools for building things. Building disciples who look like Jesus requires certain tools. Let's look at some of the tools needed in the disciple-maker's toolbox.

The first tool needed for disciple making is **the Holy Spirit**. Trying to make disciples without the power of the Holy Spirit is like trying to cut an inch-thick piece of metal with your bare hands. You need a power tool to cut a piece of metal, and you need the power of God's Spirit to transform a life into the image of Christ. If you are involved in a disciple-making relationship, pray that the Holy Spirit will be at work in that disciple's life.

The next tool needed in disciple making is **the truth of God**. Trying to make disciples without the Bible is like trying to build a wall without a level. The truth of God is the measuring rod for life. God's Word keeps us straight and level. When it comes to making disciples who look like Jesus, I have found that teaching the life of Christ is the key. If you are committed to making disciples who look like Jesus, show your disciples the life of Christ in the Scriptures.

A third tool you need in making disciples is **the people of God**. Trying to make disciples without solid relationships is like trying to put two pieces of wood together without nails, screws, or glue. God often uses people as the means by which His truth and His Spirit operate in your life. Remember what Solomon says in Proverbs 27:17, *"As iron sharpens iron, so one man sharpens another."*

The Holy Spirit makes disciples by transforming us with God's Word in the context of relationships. That is the formula for making a complicated project much simpler. Making disciples might not be easy, but it does not have to be complicated. If you have the tools God gives you in your toolbox, you are ready to make disciples who look like Jesus. It really is all about being smarter than what you are working with.

Day Thirty-Six:
"Prayership"

I must admit, every time I make the commitment to invest in a group of men through a discipleship relationship, I have reasonably high expectations. I like to think that spending a year or two with a handful of guys will result in men who are Bible expositors, evangelistic champions, off-the-chart church leaders, and multiplying machines.

A serious reality check hits me about a week or two after I begin meeting with my potential spiritual superheroes. The reality actually hits me the first time we pray together in our group. In almost every discipleship group I have ever led, at least one person is hesitant to pray out loud. Some guys are flat-out petrified at the thought of praying in a group. When this prayer paralysis strikes, I begin to realize that the most significant thing that might happen in a person's life is that he learns how to pray. It has dawned on me many times that discipleship is often prayership.

Many things can be learned in a year of meeting with a group of men. However, one of the things I think most notable is the growth I see in how a person prays. Many areas of spiritual growth are hard to identify. For example, you might not easily see growth in the Word, in character, or in stewardship, but I've heard with my own ears men who go from saying, "God is great, God is good," to calling down fire from heaven.

I remember one man who was terrified to pray when we started our weekly meetings. His standard answer during our group prayer time was the word, "Pass." Slowly but surely over the course of the next year, we nudged him into a level of comfort in praying with his fellow disciples. A few years later, I was in a prayer circle with him, and I could hardly believe my ears. This man was praying like Billy Graham!

Over years of investing in people's spiritual growth, I have begun to see that prayer is a good outward indicator of many other areas of spiritual development. It is in many ways like cross training. When an athlete trains in one area, benefits are reaped in other areas. When I lift weights with my legs, my upper body also develops. When a person grows in his prayer life, he will very likely grow in his knowledge of God's Word, his ability to share his faith, and other areas of his faith journey. Prayer is not the total evidence of spiritual growth but is definitely one indicator that God is doing something in a person's life.

Even Jesus made the teaching of prayer a priority with his disciples. Can you imagine their first prayer meeting together? I wonder if Peter said, "pass," or if John squeezed Andrew's hand as an indication that he wasn't planning to pray. At some point, even Jesus realized the men He would leave in charge of His movement needed to learn how to pray. That is exactly why Jesus said in Luke 11:2, *"When you pray, say: ..."*

Always remember that a great discipleship group is a prayership group. You may teach an incredible lesson, but don't forget to pray. You may have to cut the group meeting short one week, but don't cut out the prayer. You may not multiply a reproducer until you reproduce a pray-er. Don't underestimate the role of prayer in making a disciple of Christ.

Day Thirty-Seven:
"Praying your A,B,C's"

Have you ever heard the story of the little girl who was kneeling beside her bed to pray when her mother overheard her saying the alphabet? When the mother asked her what she was doing the girl said, "I didn't know what to say so I just prayed my a,b,c's and let God put the words together."

If we agree that God has called us to build disciples and that part of the process is meeting together to pray, then we must think about the different ways we can teach and experience prayer.

In Luke 11:1 the Bible says, *"One day Jesus was praying in a certain place. When He finished, one of His disciples said to Him, 'Lord, teach us to pray, just as John taught his disciples.'"* This verse makes it very clear that Jesus taught His disciples how to pray. They saw Him pray, and that developed a hunger within them to do the same. I wonder how many people are hungering to pray because of the way they see me pray.

I have discovered that one of the best ways to build prayer into the life of your discipleship group is through variety. Yes, variety is the spice of life, and that is true for prayer. A little variety in prayer can go a very long way. Here are some simple and yet very practical ways you can spice up the prayer times in your group.

Make time to do a prayer walk together. Most of the people in your group have probably never taken a prayer walk, so share this great prayer experience with them. This activity gives them a great new way to pray. You might want to walk through a neighborhood praying for people who live in those homes, or you might want to walk through your church buildings or around the church property praying for the ministry. Some of the most intimate prayer times I have experienced with men I have discipled have come when taking a prayer walk.

Spend some time praying on your knees. My experience is that most people don't change the posture of prayer very often. I can't explain it, but there is something very powerful about a group of men or women all kneeling down together as they pour out their hearts to God.

Have an all-praise prayer time. At times, I have challenged my discipleship group to pray nothing but praises to God for who He is and what He has done. You will quickly notice how hard this activity is.

Some guys will slip right back into request mode, and some will run out of things to say in a hurry. Once the group gets the hang of it, you will be surprised how an all-praise prayer time boosts a person's growth in prayer.

Teach a conversational style of praying. One of my favorite ways to pray in a group setting is in a conversational format. Instead of each person praying through their entire prayer separately, this method allows each person to pray shorter prayers that makes one collective prayer to the Father. As each group member takes turns praying multiple times, you will be amazed at how much more engaging this type of prayer time can be.

Obviously, these suggestions are only the tip of the iceberg. I encourage you to think of other ways you can teach your disciples to pray. Finding fresh and creative methods for connecting with God will give you an environment of intimacy with the Lord that is a big part of the disciple-making process.

Day Thirty-Eight:
"The Not All Request Prayer Time"

Making disciples and teaching people how to pray go hand in hand. That was true for Jesus, Paul, and it is true for you and me. As we meet together to equip people to become fully trained followers of Christ, prayer becomes an essential ingredient.

Making prayer a part of a discipleship group always makes for an interesting time together. The minute you ask for prayer requests you never know what people will say. In most cases, however, the prayer request times I've experienced have a tendency to become "pray for all the sick people" times. Please do not misunderstand me. I am all for praying for those who are sick—especially if I'm sick! We need to pray for those who are ill and going through difficult times in life. I simply want to suggest that praying for those who are sick will not be the only thing on my prayer list.

I have been in a countless number of small groups during my life and heard thousands of prayer requests made for sick people. I've prayed for thousands of people's aunts, uncles, cousins, nieces, nephews, and even their dogs. These have been important prayer times, and I've seen God answer those prayers many times. Praying for the sick and infirmed is important, but that's not all there is to a great prayer time.

Years ago, I heard someone describe the prayer time in a small group as "praying your burdens." He went on to say, "If you are not praying about it, don't ask the rest of us to pray about it." That may sound like a strong statement, but the point is clear. When we truly connect with God in prayer, we need to pray heartfelt prayers. We need to pray about the things that burden us. We need to be open and honest in our prayers. We need to share prayer requests that come from the heart; not simply things we are not even praying about ourselves.

In Psalm 62:8 David says, *"Trust in Him at all times, O people; pour out your hearts to Him, for God is our refuge."* Praying your burdens to God is actually praying your heart to God. The goal of prayer in a discipleship group is not to make up things to pray about, nor to dig up a "real" need that you feel comfortable sharing, but is not too personal. The goal is to pour out your heart to God!

If you were to ask me what I am burdened about today, I could share a number of responses. I am burdened for several people who do not know Christ. I am burdened about how I am handling certain temptations and struggles in my life. I am burdened for concerns in my family. I am burdened for a few people I know who are struggling in their marriage. I am burdened for some people who might die if God doesn't heal them. I am burdened for people I know who are struggling with sin. I am burdened for the growth of our church and the personal growth of my friends. I could go on and on, but I think you get my point.

I believe there is a difference between "burden praying" and "fluff praying." I know such a comment puts me on shaky ground with some people. Obviously you cannot know a person's heart, and I cannot determine what "fluff stuff" is. All I am saying is this: when we pray with our disciples, let's pray with passion. Jesus prayed with His disciples and with passion. If Aunt Betty is your burden, pray your heart out. If you are not praying for Aunt Betty, maybe you should, and maybe her condition ought to burden us all. Our burdens should be determining our prayers.

Day Thirty-Nine:
"The Ten-Year Answer"

You may remember from Day Four the story about a discipleship group that I led with three other men at a local Chick-fil-A restaurant. The four of us met together every Friday morning to share life together and hold each other accountable for our spiritual growth. We met each week for a year and had the same waitress the entire year. She was a very spunky waitress with whom we jabbed and joked each week and had lots of fun picking on each other.

During our time at this restaurant, we often prayed for our waitress. Sometimes we prayed for her during our blessing, and sometimes we prayed for her at the end of our group time. I'm sure all of us even prayed for her on our own during our private prayer times. Our group not only prayed for this young lady, but we also invited her to church. As we built a relationship with her over the weeks, we began to know more about her life and even her spiritual condition. It became apparent that she did not attend church on a regular basis and perhaps did not even have a personal relationship with Christ.

The last day we met at the restaurant we decided to give our waitress a small gift. We had all pitched in and bought her a devotional book in some type of gift pack. We signed a thank you card and gave it to her as we prepared to leave that morning. She was very appreciative and surprised by the gift, and I believe might have even shed a tear as we thanked her for taking such good care of us. Leaving the restaurant that morning I had a good feeling about the way we had demonstrated God's love to that woman. I knew she had experienced an expression of love that was very different, and I knew she had been prayed for more than any other waitress I knew. I did *not* know what would happen ten years later.

If I were Paul Harvey this is where I would say, "And now for the rest of the story." Ten years after giving the gift to our favorite waitress, she walked into the church where I am Pastor. I couldn't believe it. I had only seen her two times in ten years, and now she was coming to our church. She had married a man whose father was a member in our church, and they decided to come and check things out. They enjoyed the services and began attending every week.

At the end of the first year of attending our church, my waitress friend and her husband attended our membership class. During the class, each person is encouraged to share their testimony of how they came to faith in Christ. My waitress friend was unable to share a story. Several leaders in the class were concerned with her spiritual condition and offered to talk with her individually about where she stood in relationship to God. The following week my waitress friend and her husband asked if we could set up a time to meet. During our time together, she opened her heart to Christ and accepted him as her Savior and Lord.

As I prayed for my new sister in Christ that night, my mind was flooded with thoughts about the power of prayer and the faithfulness of God. I thought about the way God used our discipleship group to witness the love of Christ to her. God had heard and answered our prayers. We had not seen this young lady for ten years, but she had never fallen off God's radar screen. After ten years, God answered our prayers. It reminded me of what John says in 1 John 5:14-15, *"This is the confidence we have in approaching God: that if we ask anything according to His will, He hears us. And if we know that He hears us — whatever we ask — we know that we have what we asked of Him."*

Day Forty:
"The Unforgettable Prayer Walk"

In the Day 37 lesson, I mentioned the importance of taking prayer walks as a part of the disciple-making experience. There is just something fresh and different about walking and praying as a way of connecting with God. I recommend it for every discipleship group.

After I wrote the lesson on prayer walking, I decided to do that very thing with my discipleship group the next time we met. Our meeting was only a few days later, and the excitement of leading my group in a prayer walk was more than I could stand. As we started the group I took just a minute to debrief the lesson. The lesson was on prayer, and everyone had been thinking and learning about prayer all week. I asked everyone to give me one "take away" from the lesson. As soon as each person had shared their insight from the lesson, I divided our group into pairs and instructed them to take a prayer walk through certain areas of our church campus.

I asked two guys to go outside and pray as they walked through the parking lot. I asked them to pray for God to send people to our church and to send us into our community. I sent two other guys upstairs and asked them to pray for each classroom as they walked through the hallway. I took two guys and went into our church offices and auditorium where we prayed for staff members and our worship services. The experience was an awesome one which I highly recommend.

When we all came back together, I could hardly wait to hear everyone's thoughts about the prayer walk. Some very cool things were shared, and I could tell that this experience had been a new expression of prayer for most of the guys in the group. The two guys who prayed through the parking lot couldn't wait to share their experience. I knew something interesting was about to be unpacked.

The guys from the parking lot began to share how they had been praying for God to bring people to our church when all of a sudden a lady drove up to them and asked if we were having services that evening. They told her that we did not have a Sunday evening service but invited her to come back for a morning service and check out the church. She was very appreciative of their invitation, told them she was new in the community, and would certainly visit sometime soon. As she talked, one of the guys sensed she was struggling a bit. He asked if there was anything they could pray for her about. She mentioned that she was going through some tough times and would very much appreciate their prayers. Right there on the spot one of the guys prayed for this lady. With a tear on her cheek, she thanked them for the prayer.

As the woman prepared to drive off she stopped and said to the guys, "Would it be okay if I gave you a check for the offering? While I have been moving, I have not been able to give."

At that point they handed me the check. I was quite blown away by the experience and said, "Okay boys, I think the Lord is calling us to go walk again!" Some things never change.

The whole experience I just described left me with so many different applications. I know the Lord had those guys in the parking lot for that lady, but I also believe He had the lady there for them. I know that God answered their prayers, and I know their prayers grew them. As I net it all out, one thing comes to mind. 1 Thessalonians 5:17 says it like this, *"...pray without ceasing..."* (NASB).

Day Forty-One:
"In Your Business"

One of the most important elements to a disciple-making relationship is accountability. When a group of men or women agrees to challenge each other and check up on each other, good things happen.

I can testify to the fact that because of accountability, I have memorized more verses of the Bible. I will admit I have been more intentional in my witnessing because I have been held responsible. At times, I have been more sensitive to the needs of my family because someone will be checking on that area of my life. I have been much more consistent in my quiet times and in my stewardship because someone loved me enough to hold me answerable for what I did in those areas.

Putting a value on the importance that accountability relationships have had in my life is hard to do. I can't measure how much of an impact these relationships have had on my life and can't imagine where I would be without them. In fact, I don't really even know what it feels like to not live in accountability. Sometimes my life has had formal accountability relationships, and at times it's been more informal. Either way, I am thankful God has given me a life full of people who care enough to "get in my business."

Giving someone permission to "get in your business" is one of the most important aspects of spiritual growth and development. When you willingly invite another person into your life to help hold you accountable for the things you want to be true in your life, you have taken a huge step. The key phrase is "willingly invite."

I remember a time years ago when I attempted to hold a group of men accountable without being "willingly invited." The group was a disaster. I had a leadership relationship with a group of men in the church where I served, and I thought it would be a great idea if we would continually check on each other. After about three meetings I realized this group was going nowhere fast. Nothing is worse than trying to hold people accountable when they are not willing.

I have learned the hard way that accountability for spiritual growth must be wanted. Without the desire to be held responsible for growth, the disciple-making relationship is in jeopardy and reminds me of that old adage, *"rules without relationship equals rebellion."*

I might not want to hear what you have to say, but if I know you love me, I won't mind if you get into my business. If you love me, I will accept your holding me accountable. If you are attacking me, I might resist it. You can't get into somebody's business until you have earned the right to do so.

The Scriptures give a perfect picture of the power of accountability in Galatians 2:11. The passage says, *"When Peter came to Antioch, I opposed him to his face, because he was clearly in the wrong."* Peter and Paul had a relationship with each other in which they had both shared the revelation of taking the gospel message to the Gentiles. This relationship gave them permission to hold each other accountable. Paul's love for Peter caused him to confront him. Peter's love for Paul allowed him to get into his business.

Whom are you allowing access into your life? Do you have someone who holds you accountable for the things of God in your life? Are you inviting them to get into your business?

Day Forty-Two:
"Long-Haul Accountability"

Have you ever sharpened a knife? I remember when my dad taught me how to sharpen my Cub Scout knife. He bought me a sharpening stone, put a little oil on the blade, and showed me how to slide the edge of the blade against the stone until it was sharp.

Sharpening my knife blade took time. The blade wasn't sharp after one slide down the stone. Multiple swipes were required for the blade to be sharp enough to cut the hair off the back of your arm. Cutting the hair off the back of your arm was my dad's test for how sharp a knife was. I can't tell you how many times throughout the years I have tested knife blades out by seeing how much hair they could cut off the back of my arm. There are just some things you can only learn from a father!

When I think about my life, I want to be a "back of the arm hair-cutting disciple." Now you have probably never heard of a Christ follower described in those terms. Most people don't think about being a back of the arm hair-cutting disciple, but they do want to become one.

Most believers I know truly desire to be sharpened followers. They want their lives to count, and they want their walk with God to be razor sharp. Think about it. Who accepts Christ and then desires to stay dull in their spiritual development? Nobody does! When people come to faith in Christ, they begin their spiritual journey with the desire to grow and get sharper in the spiritual things of life.

God wants all of His disciples to get sharper in their knowledge of the Scriptures. God wants all of us to have cutting-edge relationships. God wants us to have sharpness in ministry and service for Him. God never wants us to be dull in our worship or in our experience with Him. God wants us to live "back of the arm hair-cutting" lives.

So what does it take to get sharper in your spiritual development? I believe one of the things we need is long-haul accountability. Long-haul accountability is having someone in your life for years at a time who is willing to help sharpen you. Do you remember reading in Proverbs 27:17, *"As iron sharpens iron, so one man sharpens another"*?

When I spend consistent time week in and week out with a small group of fellow disciples who love me, care for me, and want to see God bring out the best in me, I will get sharper! I can't truly measure the cumulative effect this type of accountability has had on my life. I do know I wouldn't want to know what my life would have been like without it.

So what about your life? Are you getting sharper? Is your spiritual edge able to cut the hair off the back of your arm? In other words, are you making an impact for Christ in the world? I encourage you to always keep a few fellow disciples in your life who will hold you accountable for the things that matter. We all need a person like Timothy, as Paul describes him in 1 Thessalonians 3:2, *"We sent Timothy, who is our brother and God's fellow worker in spreading the gospel of Christ, to strengthen and encourage you in your faith."* Paul could have just said, "We are sending Timothy to you, our back of the arm hair-cutting brother. He will hold you accountable and help you get sharper in your walk with God." You get the point, don't you?

Day Forty-Three:
"Diligent Disciple Making"

First Timothy 4:15 says, *"Be diligent in these matters; give yourself wholly to them, so that everyone may see your progress."* Today, I had a chance to see this passage of Scripture come to life. Here is how it happened.

You may remember from Day Four that ten years prior to the time of this writing, I met with a group of three men every Friday morning for discipleship to share life together. We would discuss the Scriptures, hold each other accountable for our spiritual development, and pray together. It was a great time, and each man grew tremendously in his relationship with God.

At the end of a year of meeting together in a Chick-fil-A restaurant, we each went out and recruited a handful of guys in whom to multiply our disciple-making efforts. In a few years, we had over a hundred guys meeting weekly in discipleship groups. Seeing God produce fruit from our efforts to reproduce disciples was awesome.

Over the years, the discipleship groups, which came out of this small group of men, have decentralized and are spread out in many different times and places. I cannot even begin to tell you how many men continue to be trained as disciples because of the commitment to multiply from that Friday morning group. Measuring the progress of our efforts is impossible, and only in eternity will we know how many lives have been impacted by our commitment to multiply more disciples.

I might never fully see the progress of the disciple-making effort of our group until I get to heaven; however, I do know that at least one of those men is still very *diligent in these matters*. He is living out 1 Timothy 4:15 and is *giving himself wholly* to the Great Commission.

I know this to be true because I have personally observed his *progress*. I was on my way to meet with a handful of men at 6:30 on a Friday morning when I decided to get some chicken biscuits at the local Chick-fil-A restaurant. As I stopped at the drive-through window, I noticed one of the men from our discipleship group from ten years earlier meeting with two other guys for discipleship. Now that is *being diligent!*

Joy welled up inside as I saw this man continuing the process of multiplying disciples that we committed to ten years before. Honestly, I know very few people who have made even one disciple, much less given ten years of their life to doing so.

We live in a world where diligence is a dying character trait. Few people stick with anything for ten years, and rarely do you find someone who is willing to make disciples for ten years. We may not see the progress of a ten or twenty year commitment to disciple making until we enter eternity. That's okay. Just think how exciting it is going to be when someone comes up to you in heaven and thanks you for making an investment in someone, which years later trickled down to his or her life.

Give yourself wholly to the very thing to which Jesus wholly gave Himself. Be diligent in making disciples of Jesus Christ. Discipleship may not be the latest and greatest program going through your church, nor may it be the hottest thing in the Christian world. Discipleship is not the coolest new "Bible study" on the market, but it is doing what Jesus did! Be diligent in the same matters in which Jesus was diligent. Give yourself wholly to these matters, and somebody might just drive by and see your progress.

One footnote to this lesson: Two days before seeing my buddy leading discipleship that morning, I took my daughter to breakfast at the same restaurant. There I saw a guy leading a discipleship group that came out of a second-generation group from our original group of four. May God give us even more diligent disciple makers!

Day Forty-Four:
"The Katie's Connection"

I had an interesting experience recently. An elder, a staff person from our church, and I went to eat lunch at a country-cooking buffet restaurant named Katie's in the town of LaGrange, several miles from where I work and live. The guy who is the elder works in this town, and he invited us to have lunch with him at this particular restaurant.

I must tell you I took seriously the word "all" in the "all you can eat" sign located at the entrance. I had a stack of food on my plate: fried chicken, okra, green beans, fried green tomatoes, creamed corn, squash casserole, and blackberry cobbler. I'll spare you the details of what I had on my second plate! Let's just say too many trips to Katie's would give me an expanded waistline.

The real story about the Katie's connection is what happened after we stuffed our bellies. While the three of us were backing out of our parking space, a guy from Katie's came out of the restaurant flagging us down. My first thought was that one of us had left something on the table, or that my fellow staff member had not paid as he said he would. The man approached my truck, and I rolled down the window. He saw that I was wearing a t-shirt with our church's name on it and asked if that is where I go to church. When I told him yes, he asked if my name was Ken Adams. I told him I was, and he then mentioned that a group of people meets in the restaurant each week to do Impact Discipleship. He had made the connection between the name of our church and the discipleship course with my picture on the back cover.

I was quite excited to hear about another disciple-making point in the world where people are learning to walk as Jesus walked. I am so glad to know that the Impact resources are being used to bring God glory by challenging people to be and build disciples of Christ; plus we now have a new caterer for our next Impact banquet. I mean, disciple making and food are always a good match!

As we drove away from Katie's, the elder in our bunch said, "I can't believe I'm riding with a celebrity." I told him he had better hush or we wouldn't buy him lunch anymore.

A couple of days after our connection at Katie's, something dawned on me. I realized my elder friend was the real hero for Christ. He was the true celebrity. You see, this guy's name is Tim, the man I introduced on Day Six. Tim started an Impact Discipleship group when he began working in the town of LaGrange several years earlier. The Impact group at Katie's is fruit from his labor. Tim could say as Paul said in Philippians 1:22, *"If I am to go on living in the body, this will mean fruitful labor for me."* The people in that group don't even know who Tim is, but they know who Jesus is!

Disciple making is all about pointing people to Jesus, not us. You know you have been a faithful and fruitful disciple maker when you meet people who are growing in Christ because of your efforts, and they don't even know who you are. Something about that statement just sounds right doesn't it? When you are investing your life in such a way that disciples of Christ are being made whom you don't even know, you are walking as Jesus walked.

Are you being faithful to the process of disciple making? How much "fruitful labor" has been birthed through your life? Are you living your life today so that you will have a Katie's connection in heaven?

Day Forty-Five:
"One is a Lonely Number"

Back in the seventies, the rock group *Three Dog Night* wrote a song with the lyrics, "One is the loneliest number that you'll ever do..."

Back in the year 935 B.C. Solomon said something very similar in the book of Ecclesiastes. In chapter 4 verse 9 the Bible says, *"Two are better than one, because they have a good return for their work:..."*

God has created us out of relationship and for relationship. As part of God's plan for our relationships, He created a concept called accountability. The American Heritage Dictionary defines the word "accountability" as *being answerable, capable of being explained.* I believe God created the idea of discipleship so that the perfect environment could exist in our lives for accountability.

As I have met in small groups with men over the years, I have been held accountable for the important things in my life. I have been answerable for my walk with God, for my role as a husband and a father, and for my priorities and behavior. I could go on and on about the way a discipleship group has helped me to explain my life's actions.

The discipleship groups in which I have participated have helped me read my Bible more consistently, memorize Scripture, share my faith, go on dates with my wife, spend time with my kids, and closely watch my integrity. The accountability I have received in discipleship has helped me stay motivated in my quiet times, be a better steward, keep my thought life in check, and serve God with my gifts. The weekly checkups of accountability I've had over the years have made me give an answer for my attitude, my actions, and my attributes.

Now let me see, which of the above did I not need? I guess Solomon had it right, *"two are better than one."*

If you were to ask me how to build a disciple, I would recommend the element of accountability. I would suggest that in your connection with those you disciple, you make a time for accountability. You can have questions that bring out accountability, or you can ask each person to share for what they would like to be held accountable. There is no right or wrong way to hold someone accountable as long as it is done in the context of love.

Loving accountability is what makes a discipleship relationship so special. Accountability in a discipleship relationship is proactive when you have invited someone to come into your life and to ask you to give an answer for your actions. In discipleship, you are asking for accountability *before* you do something wrong, not because you *have* done something wrong. Accountable relationships in discipleship are positive and preventive.

When I ask someone to be my workout partner, I have invited him to hold me accountable for my physical development. Accountability in my workouts is a very positive thing because I need someone to push me in my workouts. Accountability in working out is also preventive since my workout partner prevents me from missing workouts or not working hard enough. Two have always been better than one when it comes to my workouts.

Not only is one a lonely number in working out, but one is also a lonely number in living life. God has created us to do life in relationships with accountability. I hope you are living in an environment where you are taking seriously your responsibility to hold others to their commitments as well as allowing others to hold you to yours.

Day Forty-Six:
"Change Agents"

"Do you have any addictions in your life that are controlling you rather than being controlled by God?" He hated that question, but it helped a man in my discipleship group overcome a lifelong habit of chewing tobacco.

The question, "Are you treating your wife as well as you treat others?" made one guy in my group squirm like a worm. In time, he slowly began to share stories of how his relationship with his wife was changing.

I think he wished he had never asked us to hold him accountable for his workouts. But one guy in a discipleship group from years past takes better care of his body because we loved him enough to ask him how he was doing with his exercise goals.

A guy in one of my discipleship groups started taking his children to breakfast once a week after he shared his desire to spend more quality time with his kids. He had asked us to hold him accountable for having intentional time with them.

I remember well the man in our discipleship group who began serving in a ministry of our church because he knew God wanted him to use his spiritual gift in ministry. He asked the group to not let up on him until he had found a place to serve.

It was an exciting day when a man in our discipleship group shared about leading a co-worker to faith in Christ. We all shared his enthusiasm, because he had invited the group to hold him accountable for sharing his faith at work.

A man struggling with temptation was asked if he had given in again. This weekly accountability question was standard for a man who asked us to hold him accountable for the lust of the eyes.

Two of the guys in our discipleship group admitted they were not being faithful to God with their tithe. They wanted to give more to the Lord so they asked the rest of the guys in the group to hold them accountable from time to time for doing so.

Which of these true-life stories are not "yeah God" stories? Every one is praise to God because they represent spiritual victories in people's lives. These are all real stories of real people who have been changed by God through accountability in a discipleship group.

Over the years, I have learned that when you get the Word of God, the Spirit of God, and the people of God together, lives can be changed. I know of no other environment where all three work better than in a small group of men or women who are committed to holding each other accountable for their spiritual development.

God uses us as agents for change when we meet together for God's purposes. As Hebrews 10:24 says, *"And let us consider how we may spur one another on toward love and good deeds."*

How could anyone find fault with the way God has used these discipleship relationships to change lives? Why would anyone not want to be in a discipleship group if they could see God change lives the way it has been described? If accountability in discipleship groups is an effective way to spur one another on toward love and good deeds, why wouldn't everybody want to be in a discipleship group?

Day Forty-Seven:
"Two-and-a-Half to Three Years"

A few years ago, I had the opportunity to meet with a team of people from a large publishing company to present the Impact Discipleship resources God has allowed me to develop. It was an interesting experience. They brought me into a nice boardroom and gave me about two hours to explain the disciple-making concepts behind the Impact curriculum.

Once I completed my explanation of the curriculum, any of the twelve to fifteen people in the room were free to ask me questions about the resources. These people represented different departments in the publishing company, from adult education departments to seminar and event departments. They asked some very good questions.

I answered most in a way that I felt to be satisfactory. That is until one individual asked if I thought we could repackage the materials into a shorter time frame. He felt like people in today's "market" would not give twelve weeks to each of the four parts of the Ministry Training curriculum.

You might be able to imagine the inner reaction I had to this individual's comments. If not, let me paint a picture of what was going on inside my head. First, the word "market" drove me up the wall. I understand that a publishing company is a business, and they have to sell a product. I just don't think Jesus had profits in mind when He invested two-and-a-half to three years with His twelve disciples. I am struggling to work very hard at balancing the idea of marketing discipleship materials and developing materials that help people "make disciples."

A second frustration for me was the suggestion that we need to change the disciple-making process to fit the trends of current culture. If our thirty-minute sitcom culture is not willing to spend a year in a small disciple-making context, do we change the process to accommodate the culture? Would Jesus cut short the two-and-a-half to three year investment He made with His disciples to fit their schedules?

I bet now you can sense how I was feeling on the inside while maintaining composure on the outside. I felt like asking this individual that if Jesus took two-and-a-half to three years to make disciples who would reach all nations, why does he think he can do it in four to six weeks? I did not say any of what I was feeling, but it didn't matter. They did not publish the materials anyway.

Guess what? *You* must be my market! At least you bought this book, and I hope you agree with some of what I am saying: that disciple making takes time!

Jesus shows us that making a fully trained disciple takes a serious investment of our time. I am not nearly the teacher Jesus is, and I still have trouble making a two-and-a-half to three-year investment in anyone. Jesus even spent most of every day with His disciples for a three-year period. I might meet with the guys I am investing in once a week. How much life change happens in the course of four to six weeks?

In Mark 3:13 the Bible says, *"Jesus went up on a mountainside and called to Him those He wanted, and they came to Him."* Jesus was willing to make a significant investment of time in a handful of individuals. He sacrificed His time, and they were willing to sacrifice their time. Imparting and equipping a person to be a disciple and to build more disciples takes time. The question is simple. Are you willing to give that kind of time?

Day Forty-Eight:
"A Non-Leader Leader"

I spent an entire year investing in a man who had no hint of leadership ability. He was an introvert—quiet, shy and reserved. He was really bashful and hesitant. He was steady, but being in the second seat fit him well. Let me spell it out for you. Nothing in this man said "leader material."

As the end of our discipleship group approached, I began challenging each of the men to recruit some guys and start a new discipleship group. I immediately knew this was going to be a stretch for my buddy. Each time I discussed leading a group with these guys, my non-leader friend would smile and nod in agreement with the strategy. With every nod he made I thought to myself, *"He's not going to do it, not in a million years."*

Months and months went by and my introverted, non-leader friend had made no progress whatsoever at reproducing another group of disciples. I was nearing the finish of another group of disciples when I had the shock of a lifetime. I had been completely wrong. Months after casting the vision for reproducing disciples, my non-leader friend came to me with astonishing news. He stopped me at church one day and informed me that he was about to start leading (catch that word— "leading") a discipleship group of middle-school boys.

My non-leader disciple was ready to be a leader! Watching this guy invest his life in a small group of young men was awesome. While he was intimidated by leading adults, he was a perfect match for a group of young boys. They loved following this "non-leader's" leadership.

When Jesus told His disciples to "make disciples of all nations," He did not qualify that command. Jesus did not say "go make disciples" if you have the gift of leadership. He did not say "go make disciples" if you have the gift of teaching. Jesus was saying, if you are a disciple, then "go make disciples." How can we reach all nations if only those with teaching or leadership gifts make disciples?

Over the years, I have seen dozens of individuals who did not have teaching or leadership gifts make incredible investments in building disciples. You see, the only real qualification for building a disciple is being a disciple. You don't have to have a seminary degree to make a disciple. You don't have to be a paid minister to make a disciple. In fact, in Acts 4:13 Jesus' disciples were described as *"...unschooled, ordinary men...who had been with Jesus."*

Jesus is a master at taking non-leader type individuals and using them to impact multiple generations of disciples. Jesus can take a person with no leadership giftedness or teaching ability and use him to equip another individual to live as a disciple. The key isn't ability. The key is availability.

The next time you think you don't have the ability to make a disciple, think again. The next time you challenge someone to make a disciple who doesn't think he can, give him this lesson. The disciples did not look at Jesus on the mountainside after hearing the Great Commission and say, "Oh well, we would if we had the gift of teaching."

Day Forty-Nine:
"Problem Child"

My first job after graduating with a Bachelors degree in Education was teaching physical education in an elementary school. It didn't take long to realize that I was more than a physical education teacher. I discovered that when the principal was gone, I would be called on to administer disciplinary action, because in those days you could actually paddle a child in a public school.

I remember one child in this school who was consistently in trouble. He was considered by all involved as the "problem child." Nobody knew what to do with him, and nothing seemed to change his behavior. By all accounts, he caused trouble everywhere he went. He caused trouble in the classroom, the lunchroom, and even the bathroom.

Many years after my teaching days, I discovered that problem children never go away; they simply grow up. Problem children eventually become problem adults who want things their way. They can't stay focused on a task, continually disrupt group, don't meet expectations, and in general cause trouble for everyone. I have had plenty of problem adults in discipleship groups throughout the years. I've had disciples who didn't do what they agreed to do and others who dominated the group time making everyone else wish they had stayed at home. I've had group members who were in constant conflict with other members as well as members who were doing things outside of group that were not God-honoring.

The one thing that has always encouraged me in dealing with problem disciples is the fact that Jesus had them as well. Jesus had disciples who gave Him fits, did not meet His expectations, argued with one another, got on His nerves, and even one who sold Him out to the enemy. At least I've never had a group member betray me with a kiss that led me to a cross.

In Luke 8:25 Jesus asked His disciples, *"Where is your faith?"* Luke 9:46 says, *"An argument started among the disciples as to which of them would be the greatest."* Jesus told His disciples a parable in Luke 18:1 to show them *"they should always pray and not give up."* In Luke 22:4 the Scripture says, *"And Judas went to the chief priests and the officers of the temple guard and discussed with them how he might betray Jesus."*

Finally Luke 22:61 states, *"The Lord turned and looked straight at Peter. Then Peter remembered the word the Lord had spoken to him: 'Before the rooster crows today, you will disown me three times.'"*

Wow! Jesus certainly had His problem disciples, didn't He? Should we be surprised when we experience the same problems Jesus had? If we are walking as Jesus walked, we ought to be experiencing some of the same problems Jesus experienced. If you dare to be a disciple maker, you will have to deal with difficult disciples.

Difficult disciples can make the priority of building disciples a challenge, but you don't simply give up on them. You can't. Christ didn't give up on His problem disciples nor can we. Problem disciples have to be handled with truth and love. Jesus never stopped loving Judas, and He never stopped loving Peter. Jesus always spoke the truth even when His disciples let Him down.

I bet Peter was glad Jesus spoke the truth in love to him, and I'm sure he was very thankful the Lord never gave up on him. I bet Peter was glad his disciple maker was a patient and grace-filled teacher, and I'm sure Jesus was glad He never gave up on Peter.

Day Fifty:
"A Smooth Flight"

Have you ever been on a rough airplane flight? I have, and let me tell you, it is no fun. Everybody wants a smooth ride at 30,000 feet in the air.

Smooth air travel does not happen by accident. A good flight is the product of good planning and execution. I just love it when I receive great service, have a smooth take-off, arrive safely at my destination, land smoothly, and disembark the plane without any trouble. A smooth airplane flight is, in many ways, like a small discipleship group. Some groups go smoothly, and some are bumpy. I have been in smooth and bumpy groups, and let me tell you, the bumpy ones are no fun.

A smooth discipleship group does not happen by accident; it is the product of good planning and execution. I just love it when I sit in a group that is well led. Discipleship groups are enjoyable when the leader is prepared, knows how to direct the group, communicates effectively, and ends the group meeting successfully.

Did you know that airline personnel are constantly trained? The smooth flights happen because pilots, mechanics, gate agents, and flight attendants are continually equipped for their tasks. However, you will find little or no information on how to lead a small discipleship group. Unlike the airlines, the church does very little training on how to build disciples. The church is commissioned to make disciples of all nations, yet does very little to ensure that task is accomplished. Isn't there something wrong with this picture?

Using the airline analogy let me share a few thoughts about how to lead a smooth discipleship group. If you apply these simple concepts, most bumps can be avoided, and you'll enjoy a smooth group.

Step One: Be Prepared! Airplane flights go much better when the right things are done before the plane takes off. The same is true for a small discipleship group. When the leader is prepared, the group has fewer bumps.

Step Two: Stay Alert! Airplane flights go much better when the flight crew is alert. A pilot who wanders, flight attendants who give poor service, and mechanics who miss checkpoints make for a difficult experience. A small discipleship group leader needs to stay alert to sense God's direction, understand the needs of the group members, and concentrate on where the group is headed.

Jesus was the perfect example of a small discipleship group leader. He always knew exactly where the Father was leading Him and exactly what His disciples needed. For example, in Mark 6:31 Jesus said to His disciples, *"Come with Me by yourselves to a quiet place and get some rest."* As a leader, Jesus had the discernment to know that His disciples need time alone.

Step Three: Give Direction! Good flights happen because someone knows where the plane is going. They know when and where to take off, and they know when and where to land. I've been in some discipleship groups that didn't have a good take off, couldn't find their destination, and never landed.

I like being in a small discipleship group where the leader gives direction. Good leaders follow a map when it comes to leading a group. They know how to start a group, make good mid-flight adjustments, and when and where to land the group. As leaders, let us commit to continually work as the airlines do to ensure quality group times.

Day Fifty-One:
"The Hang Factor"

I'll be the first to admit that I am not good at it, but "the Hang Factor" is a huge part of building a disciple of Christ. I hope you don't have to be perfect at something in order to write about it because I would have to leave this chapter out of the book. I know, however, that this component of discipleship is critical, and I am striving to get better at hanging out with those I am disicipling.

"The Hang Factor" is simply spending time with those you are discipling outside of the small group time. "The Hang Factor" is all about building relationships with the individuals you are training and equipping as disciples.

Jesus had some serious hang time with His disciples. The culture Jesus lived in made "the Hang Factor" much easier to accomplish than it is today. Jesus and His disciples walked together wherever they went, which built in hang time. Jesus and His disciples did ministry together which provided them with some serious hang time. Jesus and His disciples regularly ate together. All in all, Jesus and His disciples spent a great deal of time together. Not all of this time was spent teaching, praying, or talking about ministry. Much of the time Jesus spent with His disciples was simply hanging out in-between activities.

Matthew 11:1 says, *"After Jesus had finished instructing His twelve disciples, He went on from there to teach and preach in the towns of Galilee."* The formal teaching time was over, and the informal was ready to begin. Jesus made an impact on His disciples while they traveled between cities.

Our busy lives make the priority of having relational time with those we are investing in a challenge. When you work forty to fifty hours a week, hang time is hard to come by. When you attend three of your children's ball games a week, that makes hang time difficult. When you serve on a ministry team at your church, that limits your in-between time. There is no question that making extra time for those you disciple is a hard thing to do. How do we find time to simply hang out with our disciples?

First, include your disciples in what you already do! Sometimes you are already doing things that a disciple would enjoy doing with you.

Invite those you disciple to travel with you, eat with you, and even do ministry with you. You might be surprised how many people are willing to join you in your regular activities.

Secondly, use technology to connect! Hang time can also be phone time or e-mail. A simple connection between your regular group meetings will make a huge difference in the relationship you have with your disciples. A short, simple call or message can go a long way with those you are training and equipping for ministry.

Finally, be intentional about having hang time! If you plan for hang time in your schedule, you are more likely to do it. Build into your calendar lunch time, recreational time, or ministry time in which you will connect with the person you are training.

The phrase *"more is caught than taught"* is the principle for hang time. Hang time is never wasted time, but instead becomes a strategic time for modeling who you want your disciple to become. If you are following Christ, then every second you spend with your disciple is a worthwhile investment.

Day Fifty-Two:
"Keep It Small"

Over the years, I have participated in many different types of groups in the churches where I have belonged. I have been in large group environments, medium size groups, small groups of ten to twelve, and even smaller groups of three to four. Each and every one of these groups has served different purposes in my life, and the size of the group has played a big part in accomplishing that purpose.

I am regularly asked about the best size for a discipleship group. That is a great question, and there is certainly not a "right" answer. I have seen discipleship done in groups of eight to twelve and sometimes in groups of five or six. I must say, however, that the ideal number for a discipleship group, in my mind, is three to four individuals. Even Jesus limited His time on certain occasions to a small group of three disciples. In Matthew 17:1 the Bible says, *"After six days Jesus took with Him Peter, James and John the brother of James, and led them up a high mountain by themselves."* Jesus had twelve disciples, but He spent more time with Peter, James, and John than He did the rest.

Consider the following reasons why a discipleship group should be limited to no more than four.

Reason #1: The larger the group, the less people will talk. There is no question that the amount of sharing diminishes with the increase in group size. A group of four people will always yield more heart-to-heart sharing than a group of eight people. Since discipleship is about relationship, I advocate keeping your group small to increase the amount of sharing.

Reason #2: The smaller the group, the better the care. This is a no-brainer. Checking on and caring for three people is easier than caring for nine people. The level of connection and care for a discipleship group needs to be close; the closer the connection and care, the deeper the experience. Keep your group small so you can keep your group close.

Reason #3: The smaller the group, the easier hanging out becomes. Limiting the number of people you invest in expands the amount of time you can be with those you want to equip.

Reason #4: The smaller the group, the easier group management is. Let's face it, people are busy these days, and trying to get more than three to four people together on a regular basis is a challenge. You will have a higher degree of succeeding in managing a group of three to four disciples than you will with a group of twelve.

Reason #5: A group of three to four is healthier than one-on-one. I think a one-on-one discipleship relationship is acceptable but not necessarily ideal. When there are more than two people, there is a healthier degree of accountability within the group. When you have four people in a group, it also means at least three people are present when one is absent. Investing in two or three people instead of one also increases your odds of multiplication. All in all, I recommend building disciples in groups of three to four individuals.

I once heard someone say, "You can impress a crowd, but you can only impact a few." If your desire is to have a lasting impact for Christ, keep it small!

Day Fifty-Three:
"Keep It Separate"

Every time I speak at a church on the topic of disciple making I usually get asked, "Does a discipleship group have to be 'men only' and 'women only' groups? Can you mix men and women together?"

You can tell by the title of this lesson how I answer the question of having groups with mixed gender. I always recommend keeping discipleship groups separate. Sometimes people prefer to do couples groups with husbands and wives. While I think a married couples group is okay, men and women should be separated during the meeting time. Let me give you some of my reasons for keeping groups separate.

First, keep it separate for the purpose of sharing. Men and women share things differently. Basically, women share, and men don't. Not really. Men do share, but they are usually not comfortable sharing intimate details of their lives with members of the opposite sex. Women are the same. Women are much more comfortable sharing intimate issues with women than they are with men. In a couples group, opening up might be hard for a husband or wife if his or her spouse is in the group. In a couple's group setting, I would recommend breaking up into small women's and men's groups during share time.

Second, keep it separate to eliminate tempting circumstances. I know some will scoff at this point, but I'll make it nevertheless. I have been in ministry for over twenty-five years as I write this lesson, and I wish I could say this point is not necessary. I can't. I have seen too many well-intentioned people give in to sexual temptation within the church. You do not need to set up circumstances where an emotional attachment can build. A discipleship group is just such a circumstance. If we pray, "Lord, lead us not into temptation," why would we take ourselves there?

Third, keep it separate because our needs are different. My wife tells me all the time, "Men and women relate differently in a discipleship setting." One of my buddies says, "Men like to spit and grunt, and women like to talk and sip flavored coffee." While I like a little latte myself, I certainly understand the relational differences between men and women. I once led a couples group where, for some reason, the men always finished their prayer-and-share time sooner than the women did— actually, about 30 minutes sooner. How much sharing can you do, anyway?

As always, I must take us back to Jesus as our model for disciple making. Jesus had great relationships with women, and they played a huge part in His ministry. Mark 15:41 says, *"In Galilee these women had followed Him and cared for His needs. Many other women who had come up with Him to Jerusalem were also there."* Women were very much a part of Jesus' life, but they were not in His inner circle. Jesus' inner circle of disciples was Peter, James, and John—not Paula, Jessica, and Janice! Keep it separate.

Day Fifty-Four:
"The Need for Speed"

If I have said it once, I have said it one hundred times. The speed of the leader equals the speed of the team. I don't remember the first time I heard that statement, or even who said it, but the impact it has had on my life has been incredible. The longer I lead the more I understand the importance of this truth. Building disciples requires leadership. There is absolutely no way around it. If you want to build a solid movement of disciple making, you will have to have solid leaders. The speed of your leaders will determine the speed of your team!

I believe Jesus lived by the speed of the leader principle when He commissioned His disciples to be disciple makers. He did not rush to designate His disciples as leaders. He did not commission leaders prematurely. Jesus did not raise up perfect leaders, but He did send out called and qualified leaders.

If there is one verse that demonstrates the progress of Christ's original disciples, it might be Luke 5:11: *"So they pulled their boats up on shore, left everything and followed Him."* In this one verse we see a group of men who were available, faithful, and teachable. We see men who were willing to become what Jesus wanted every one of His disciples to be.

Called and qualified leaders will always be F.A.T. leaders. They will be faithful, available, and teachable. Peter was not a perfect leader, but he was available when Christ turned him loose. John did not know everything there was to know about leadership, but he was faithful when Jesus commissioned him to make disciples. James had never been to a leadership seminar or read a book on leadership, but he was teachable when Jesus drew him to His side.

When it comes to designating a person to a leadership role, look for F.A.T. disciples. Disciples who are **faithful** will set the pace for others. People will make good leaders when you know they will do what they are asking others to do. A leader who teaches giving yet does not give is not faithful. A leader who talks about witnessing and does not witness is not faithful. A leader who talks about praying and reading the Scriptures but does not do it is not faithful. A leader who is not faithful is going to slow down those who follow.

Disciples who are **available** make good leaders. A leader who shows up to lead his group and is available to spend time with his disciples outside the group is going to set the proper pace. A leader who misses the group meetings and has no time for the people in his or her group is not qualified to lead. A person can have all the charisma in the world, but if he does not show up, he won't be a very good leader. Good leaders are available.

A called and qualified leader must remain **teachable**. As soon as a person begins to think they know it all, they are in big trouble. God uses leaders who are learners.

Day Fifty-Five:
"Grace-Based Disciple Making"

"You didn't do your lesson!"
"You didn't memorize your verse!"
"Just how many meetings are you going to miss?"
"Are you committed to this process, or not?"

How many times have you heard these kinds of statements? I have to admit that I've heard these types of comments many times, and way too often it has been in the context of a discipleship group. In fact, I know people who think the whole idea of discipleship is a legalistic concept with the misconception of thinking that any kind of commitment or accountability is legalism. I am saddened to think that discipleship can be abused in this way.

I admit that sometimes discipleship can have a legalistic tendency. I have seen more than one zealous discipleship leader go over the top on commitment and accountability, resulting in a "want to" becoming a "have to" perspective before anybody knew what happened. I've known more than one discipleship leader who has raked his group members over the coals for not keeping up their commitment to the expectations of the group. Yes, I have seen discipleship be anything but grace-based.

What kind of discipleship group do you think Jesus had? Do you think it was a grace-based group? I do. I can't imagine Jesus having anything but a grace-based approach to making disciples. Did that mean there was no accountability? Did that mean Jesus never spoke the truth or challenged His closest followers to deeper levels of commitment? Did Jesus ever give His disciples a rebuke or corrective word? In Mark 7:18 Jesus says to His disciples, *"Are you so dull?"* In Luke 9:62 Jesus says, *"No one who puts his hand to the plow and looks back is fit for service in the kingdom of God."* In Luke 14:27 Jesus says, *"And anyone who does not carry his cross and follow Me cannot be My disciple."* It appears to me Jesus had some strong words for His disciples at times. Does that mean Jesus was not a grace-based disciple maker?

Think for a moment about some of the problems Jesus had with His disciples. Did the words, *"you are so dull,"* come to mind when He found the disciples sleeping instead of praying (Mark 14:37-38)? I wonder if the *"hand to the plow"* statement came to mind when Peter denied Jesus publicly (Luke 22:54-62). How did the words *"carry his cross"* match up with Thomas when he doubted the Lord's resurrection (John 20:24-25)?

It doesn't take long to realize Jesus had balance in His disciple-making relationships. Jesus found the perfect balance between grace and truth. Jesus did not give His disciples grace so that sin might abound; instead, He spoke the truth and demonstrated favor even when it was unmerited. Jesus gave His disciples the perfect picture of how grace and truth work together.

One of our challenges in disciple making is to find the balance between grace and truth. Those whom you disciple will need you to tell them the truth, but they will also need you to give them grace. You do too, don't you?

Day Fifty-Six:
"The Bull's Eye"

I still remember the day my father brought home a dartboard for my older brother and me. I'm still surprised we have both our eyes and no body parts pierced from our dart-throwing days in the basement.

Over thirty years have passed since my dad brought home that dartboard, and I have it in my basement this very day. It does look quite a bit different now than it did some thirty odd years ago. Today it is so filled with holes that parts of the board are falling apart. In fact, the red spot in the center, the bull's eye, is completely gone.

Obviously, the bull's eye was the first piece to fall apart because that is the place everybody had been aiming for all those years. For over three decades, every person to throw a dart at that board has been aiming at the center. I've seen plenty of people hit the edge, but I've never seen anyone *aim* for the edge.

Have you ever wondered what the target is when it comes to disciple making? Do we know what we are aiming for when we invest in potential disciples? Is there any way we can measure our effectiveness in making disciples?

The answer is yes! Disciple making has a target. The bull's eye we need to aim for in the disciple-making process is Jesus!

When Jesus told His disciples to "go and make disciples," do you think they wondered what the target was? Did they think Jesus meant to make disciples like Peter, James, or John? Not at all! The original disciples knew they were to make disciples who looked just like Jesus.

Jesus is the target and our Model. We measure the effectiveness of our disciple-making efforts by how much our disciples live like Jesus lived. Even some thirty years after Christ's life, Paul said in 1 Corinthians 11:1, *"Follow my example, as I follow the example of Christ."*

Paul was not aiming at the edge, but was fixed on the right target. He had the bull's eye in his sights. Paul knew that the end product of the disciple-making process was individuals who had the same characteristics and priorities as that of Christ.

I am afraid that the target for disciple making is unclear for many people today. If you asked ten people what a disciple ought to look like, my guess is you would get ten different answers. How can that be? Over the years, the target has become very fuzzy. The past two thousand years have made the end product of disciple making very unclear for those who still believe they ought to be about the process.

At a bare minimum, the same characteristics that were true of Jesus ought to be true of His disciples. Jesus was involved in community, demonstrated identity, participated in ministry, and prioritized maturity. Those same characteristics were also true of His disciples and ought to be true of those we disciple.

If we are serious about making disciples, we must know what our target is. We must know when we have been effective and when we have missed the mark completely. I pray that we see the target so clearly that we hit it every time.

Day Fifty-Seven:
"Committed to Community"

When you look to Jesus as the end product of the disciple-making process, you see the importance of living in community. Jesus lived in community, and His disciples lived in community. The disciples of the disciples lived in community. It isn't rocket science to figure out that one of the characteristics of a disciple of Christ is being committed to community.

If Jesus and His disciples were committed to living life in the context of community, are we making true disciples of Christ if that same commitment is not shared by those we disciple? I think not.

Think of it this way. Let's say our goal is to develop a world-class athlete, and one of the characteristics of all top-notch athletes over the years has been a commitment to running. Will you have a world-class athlete if he never does any running as a part of his training regimen?

World-class athletes are known by a certain number of common characteristics. Running is one such characteristic. Disciples of Jesus Christ are also known by a certain number of common characteristics. Living in the context of biblical community is one such characteristic.

Jesus did not live in community because it was easy. He lived in community because it was the right thing to do. God has created us to be relational beings, and we are designed to live life in the context of relationships. We need other believers in our lives, and other believers need us. Jesus modeled for us the value of living life in the context of relationships so that all of His disciples would share His commitment to community.

During the time of Christ's earthly ministry, He made relationships a priority. Those relationships were at times frustrating, challenging, and disappointing. He lived life in community anyway. Jesus certainly did not need relationships to accomplish His mission, but He chose the relational approach to do so. Jesus might not have needed relationships, but He knew we would.

Living life in the context of biblical community is part of God's plan to make disciples of all nations. We are not called to live in community simply for the sake of community. We are called to live in community for the purpose of making disciples!

A small community of believers provides the relational context for the disciple-making process. In the same way Jesus lived in a small group to make disciples, we are to live in a small group in order to make disciples. In Acts 2:46 the Bible says, *"Every day they continued to meet together in the temple courts. They broke bread in their homes and ate together with glad and sincere hearts..."* The small group environment was an essential part of the disciple-making process for both Jesus and those He discipled.

The small group created the relational environment for communicating truth, experiencing fellowship, practicing ministry, and applying information. Jesus used the small group in a very strategic way.

If Christ made disciples in the context of a small group, who are we to think we don't need a small group? Do we dare think that our plan for making disciples is better than Christ's? Are we making disciples at all if the end product of the disciple-making process doesn't lead people into a life-changing small group? May every disciple we make be one who lives life committed to community!

Day Fifty-Eight:
"Prioritizing Maturity"

One thing all disciple makers can agree on is that a disciple of Jesus Christ is one who makes spiritual growth a priority in life. Just think about it. Jesus had a priority of the Scriptures and prayer in His life, and the original disciples placed a priority on the Scriptures and prayer in their lives. The disciples of the original disciples made prayer and the Word a priority in their lives. So why wouldn't disciple makers in today's world see the bull's eye of disciple making being a person who is growing spiritually?

I spent over twenty-two years gaining a formal education, and after all those years I still did not know it all. What went wrong? You would think after that much time I would have a handle on certain subjects. Obviously, I learned a great deal during my years in school, but learning all there was to know was never the objective. I went to school to learn how to learn! The objective of my education was to learn how to find the information I needed to know. My priority was growth.

When Jesus left His disciples here on earth, they did not know everything they could possibly know. They simply knew everything Jesus wanted them to know in order to accomplish His mission. Jesus gave them the value of prioritizing growth and maturity in their lives, and that value continued to develop even after Jesus was gone. Acts 2:42 says, *"They devoted themselves to the apostles' teaching and to the fellowship, to the breaking of bread and to prayer."* Jesus had successfully passed on the characteristic of spiritual growth to the next generation of disciples.

If you are making disciples of Christ who value the priority of spiritual development in their lives, and if I am making disciples of Christ who couldn't care less about the priority of spiritual development, someone is missing the mark. Someone is aiming at the wrong bull's eye. We cannot both be making disciples of Christ if those disciples don't both look like Jesus.

Even a brief overview of Christ's life reveals the priority He placed on the Scriptures and prayer. Over and over again the gospels show that Jesus made time for prayer and used the Scriptures in conversations. Jesus clearly prioritized the Word in His life and spent much time in the discipline of prayer. A disciple of Jesus Christ should prioritize the same things.

I find it interesting how many people claim to be disciples of Christ but do not prioritize the same things Christ did. You do not have to look very far to find "disciples" who never spend time in the Bible and rarely, if ever, spend time in prayer. This makes me think something is wrong with our definition of a disciple or the process we are using to make them.

The best way I know to correct the confusion we seem to have in making disciples is to start by being the right disciple. Are you a disciple who prioritizes the same things Jesus did? When was the last time you memorized a verse or quoted one in a conversation? How long has it been since you spent time in prayer and connected with the Father?

May we be disciples who do what Jesus did, and may we build disciples who prioritize the same things Jesus did!

Day Fifty-Nine:
"Demonstrating Identity"

When I was in high school, guys and girls went steady with each other. When a guy and girl were going steady, the guy would let his girlfriend wear his letter jacket and his class ring. The jacket and ring demonstrated identity and let everyone know who a girl's boyfriend was.

Disciples of Jesus Christ should demonstrate identity with Him. Our commitment to Christ should be obvious by the way we live our lives. We don't wear a ring or jacket that identifies us with Christ; instead, we demonstrate our identity with Christ through our attributes, attitudes, and actions.

When we are demonstrating identity through our attributes, it means "who we are" points people to God. If someone said, "That's just not you," they are describing the attributes you typically demonstrate as opposed to different attributes. When you are following Christ, people should see godly attributes in you!

A life that demonstrates identity points people to God through attitude. What you think determines your attitude. As a disciple of Jesus Christ, you think with the mind of Christ. When you are thinking about life the way Jesus did, you are demonstrating a godly attitude.

The actions of your life also demonstrate your identity with Christ. Your behavior, or what you do, either points people to Jesus or away from Him. When a person is behaving in a godly manner, he is identified with God.

Jesus was the perfect example of what it means to demonstrate identity. Jesus continually pointed people to the Father by who He was, what He thought, and what He did. Everything about Christ's life came from the Father, and He gave credit to the Father. In John 17:7 Jesus said, *"Now they know that everything You have given Me comes from You."* Jesus clearly identified His life with His Father.

If we are making disciples who walk as Jesus walked, they should demonstrate identification with the Father as well. All disciples should be developing attributes, attitudes, and actions that look more like Jesus and less like themselves. Do the individuals you have discipled point people to Jesus with their words, their deeds, and their personality? We are making the wrong kind of disciples if they are not decreasing while Christ is increasing in them.

The true mark of a disciple of Christ is not a gold cross worn on a chain around the neck, a fish bumper sticker on the back of the car, or by wearing a Christian t-shirt. A true disciple of Christ is known by a life that points people to God!

So who gets the credit in your life? Are your actions, attitudes, and attributes demonstrating that you are a Christ follower? If the answer to that question is no, then you are not being the disciple Christ meant for you to be. How can you build the right type of disciple if you are not being the right type of disciple? May every disciple you make be a person who demonstrates an identity with the Father!

Day Sixty:
"Participating in Ministry"

The word *ministry* simply means "meeting needs." Obviously that is what making disciples is all about. Christ commissioned us to make disciples so He would have a whole world filled with ministers who are meeting needs.

If you ask most church members how many ministers they have in their church, they will likely give you the total number of paid staff members. There is a chance someone might answer by giving you the total number of members on their church roll. That is the correct answer!

When we are making disciples of Jesus Christ, every member ought to be a minister. Every member and disciple of Christ ought to be a person who is going into all nations meeting needs.

Jesus did not make disciples simply for the purpose of community, maturity, and identity. Jesus made disciples to participate in ministry. Jesus wants His disciples to help bring people to faith and to reproduce more disciples. Those two objectives are the ultimate goals of participating in ministry.

If all Jesus had done was come to create community, the whole movement of Christianity would have come to a halt once the original group of disciples had died out. If Jesus had come to develop super-mature disciples, the movement to reach all nations would have ceased when they died off. If Jesus had only lived a life of identifying with the Father and not one of leaving behind multiplying disciples, His whole mission would eventually be aborted.

Making disciples who participated in ministry by reaching the lost and reproducing disciples ensured the success of Christ's mission. When Jesus made disciples who reached and trained more disciples, He was launching a movement of making ministers.

In Ephesians 4:11-12, Paul instructs leaders in the church to *"prepare God's people for works of service, so that the body of Christ may be built up."* I believe those works of service are ministry! The body of Christ is built up when people are reached and trained to be disciples. Jesus did the exact same thing Paul is instructing leaders in the church to do. Jesus equipped God's people, His followers, to do works of service so that the body of Christ would be built up. If that is what Jesus did in making disciples, isn't that what we are supposed to do?

How on earth can we claim to be "making disciples" if the end product is not participation in ministry? If the end result of the disciple-making process is a notebook on a shelf, we are not making disciples. If the end result of a disciple-making investment is only sweet fellowship, we are not making disciples. If the end result of the disciple-making process is only a holy lifestyle, we are falling short of making a true disciple. If, however, the end product of the disciple-making process is a disciple who is going deeper in faith, living in sweet fellowship, growing in holiness, and building more disciples who multiply, *then* we are making true disciples of Christ.

Making disciples who participated in ministry is what Jesus did. Making disciples who participated in ministry is what Jesus' disciples did. Making disciples who participate in ministry is what we are to be doing. May every disciple you make be one who is participating in the ministry of making more disciples!

Day Sixty-One:
"Disciple Making or Discipleship?"

I sent an invitation to a pastor friend of mine to attend a conference we were having at our church on disciple making. He returned the invitation with the following comment, "Sorry, we won't be able to attend the conference — we are focusing on evangelism this year in our church." My friend obviously misunderstood what I meant by a conference on disciple making. I understand my friend's confusion because I was confused myself for many years when it came to the difference between discipleship and disciple making. I always wanted to be evangelistic, but for years I separated evangelism and discipleship in my thinking.

For many years, I was a champion of discipleship. I wanted what I thought was the deeper life. I wanted to experience the spiritual disciplines in the deepest way possible and help others experience them as well. My goal was to go as deep in my relationship with God as possible and help others go there too. I was content to go deeper but not very focused on going wider.

A defining moment came for me when I heard a friend, Dann Spader, make the comment, "I like the words *disciple making* better than the word *discipleship*." That one sentence opened up a whole new world for me. I began to see discipleship and evangelism as one process. I began to realize the goal of disciple making was not simply to "go deeper;" rather the goal of disciple making is to go deeper **and wider**. For the first time in my life I realized there was no need for a conference on evangelism or discipleship. The only conference needed was one on disciple making!

When we look at the life of Christ, we see that He was committed to disciple making — not just discipleship. Jesus taught the original disciples so that they would evangelize and train other disciples. Jesus wasn't just taking twelve men deeper in the spiritual disciplines; He was training them to change the world!

Jesus took His disciples deeper so that they would go wider. I'm quite sure Jesus never taught His disciples the song "Deep and Wide" or the hand motions to go with it! He did, however, set in motion a process of spiritual development that worked. Jesus never separated evangelism from discipleship; instead, He saw those who were evangelized as becoming disciples and those who were being discipled as becoming evangelists. That is disciple making.

Luke 9:6 describes the disciples as going *"...from village to village, preaching the gospel and healing people everywhere."* The disciples were going deeper to go wider. They had been with Jesus so that they could go out and preach the gospel. Jesus never intended His disciples to just go deeper. His goal was to see them go wider as well.

What is our goal for those we disciple? Have we lost track of what disciple making really is? Are we thinking that disciple making is just inward and not outward? Disciple making is both inward and outward. That is what Jesus came to do. He came to change us on the inside so He could change the world on the outside.

The next time you get an invitation to attend a conference on disciple making, I suggest you go. Why? First, these conferences are very difficult to find. Secondly, because you can never learn too much about the plan God chose to change the world.

Day Sixty-Two:
"A Life-Changing Environment"

I am going out on a limb with this statement. I believe a small discipleship group is the best possible environment for life change to occur. When you have three to five men or women gathered together on a weekly basis for a significant period of time—one to two years—you will see the greatest amount of life change. When that small group spends time in the Scriptures, holds each other accountable, and prays together, you will see God change lives.

I have seen this life-changing environment first hand and have been fortunate enough to have a front-row seat for life change in many individuals. I have watched the Spirit of God take this disciple-making environment and use it to change attitudes, attributes, and actions. Those changed individuals went on to change marriages, families, churches, businesses, and communities. When God changes a person, change occurs in many other places.

Recently a man said, "Four years ago I didn't even know where Ecclesiastes was in the Bible. This week I read some great stuff from it." This same man is leading a small group in our church and serving as an usher in our services. Four years ago, he wasn't attending church at all.

I met a man at one of our services about four or five years ago and thought to myself, "This guy will never be back." For the past six months he has been in my discipleship group. He recently received a buy-out from the company where he worked, and the first thing he did was give 10% of his earnings to God. Even though the gift was significant, he didn't hesitate to give to God.

A man in my discipleship group for the past six months was not involved in church at all a little over a year ago. Today he is a small group leader and has been on numerous mission trips through the ministry of our church.

Two years ago I sat with a group of men that accounted for well over one hundred years of living for Christ. Of that group, not one man had ever led one other person in a disciple-making process. One of those men has since taken five men through a year of discipleship, and four of those five have now started their own discipleship groups. That is life change!

Matthew 9:9 says, *"As Jesus went on from there, He saw a man named Matthew sitting at the tax collector's booth. 'Follow Me,' He told him, and Matthew got up and followed Him."* Those two words, "follow Me," changed Matthew's life forever. Those two words were an invitation from Jesus for Matthew to join a disciple-making environment. That environment would change the course of Matthew's life.

When a man moves from being a dishonest tax collector to Christ follower, you can bet some serious life change has taken place. Isn't it amazing how the Spirit of God used the environment Christ created to change Matthew's life?

"You can impress a crowd, but you can only impact people close up." I have no idea who made that statement, but it is 100% correct. Life change happens best when three or four people are in an environment where they are close enough to make an impact. Why would we not make participating in disciple-making environments an ongoing priority in our lives?

Day Sixty-Three:
"World Changers"

I love the story of the Sunday school teacher who was feeling pretty good about the lesson she had just taught her five year old students on Jesus and His disciples. Patting herself on the back, she decided to ask the children what they had learned about discipling. One little girl started waving her hand in the air. She obviously had the right answer to her teacher's question. The little girl said, "Oh. I know a lot about discipling; at my house, we disciple everything — we disciple glass, we disciple paper and we disciple plastic. My mom says it's how we are going to save the earth!"

I think it is safe to say this little girl has the correct theology even if she has the incorrect terminology. Making disciples who will make more disciples is how Christ intended for us to save the earth.

I know there are many skeptics in the world when it comes to the idea of reaching the world by multiplying disciples. Certainly the idea of reaching two who reach four and then eight and so on will eventually break down. However, the problem is not the plan; the problem is people. Even if people prevent a pure process of multiplying disciples to occur, I will still not abandon the plan.

I know many marriages that don't work even though the plan for marriage is God's design. I have not given up on marriage because I have seen marriages break down. We all know that marriages break down because of broken people, not because of a broken plan.

Think for a minute about all the different ways we could make disciples of all nations. A few plans come to my mind immediately. We could make disciples through technology—the internet and satellite technology could be huge tools in global disciple making. Maybe we could take the approach of social activism by lobbying in the legislative arena or staging public protests to bring about change. We could continue exploring ideas for changing the world, or we could look at the approach Jesus used.

While there are many possible ideas and theories on disciple making, we only need to look to Jesus to see how He made disciples. Jesus did not create a web-based discipleship curriculum, nor did He hold a protest for change. Jesus did not write his congressman, or organize a march in the nation's capital. Jesus used a relational approach. He changed individuals and believed those individuals would help others until the entire world was changed.

I am not suggesting that letters to politicians are not important. I am not saying that technology does not have a place in disciple making. After all, I am using a computer to write this book. All I am saying is that we are only going to change the world by doing the same thing Jesus did. Jesus changed individuals, and those people changed the world.

The officials in Thessalonica were shouting that the apostles *"...who have caused trouble all over the world have now come here..."* (Acts 17:6). World changers, I believe? How did those apostles become known as world changers? How did they get the reputation of being trouble makers? The "rest of the story," as Paul Harvey would say, is in Acts 4:13. "When they saw the courage of Peter and John and realized they were unschooled, ordinary men, they were astonished and they took note that these men had been with Jesus."

Do you see it? These men changed the world because they had been changed. The disciples were individuals who experienced a life-changing relationship with Jesus Christ and in turn shared the same experience with others. Making disciples who make disciples is God's plan, and His strategy for how we are going to save the earth. Don't give up on God's plan—His plan continues to work.

Day Sixty-Four:
"Guidance Counselor"

Picture this in your mind … You are taking a first grader to school on the first day of class. You ask the teacher what she has planned for your child. She says, "I thought I would start by teaching multiplication tables and then move into fractions, then do addition and subtraction in a few months." I bet your response would be, "Not with my child"!

When you place a child in a learning environment, that setting needs to match up with his or her stage of life. You do not teach algebra or composition to a first grader. Nor do you put a second grader in an engineering class. You always place a child in an age-appropriate environment for learning.

As a disciple maker, you must see yourself, in many ways, like a guidance counselor. When I enrolled in college, I was assigned a guidance counselor who helped me chart out my academic courses through four years of college. This person did his best to help match up my academic needs with my desires for a certain degree program. I was advised on what to take first, second, and so forth.

Good disciple makers advise those they are discipling which direction to take. New believers need to be trained in the basics of the faith and to be taught basic doctrine, basic Bible, basic Christian living, and basic church life. More mature believers need to be trained to do ministry and become disciple makers. They need to be taught their life's mission, what an authentic disciple looks like, how to intentionally live their life, and how to find their place in a movement of disciple making. Once a person is equipped to be a disciple maker, he still needs to be in an environment of life-long learning. Every disciple maker needs to continue learning and growing. Never stop learning! Never stop growing! Make a commitment to be a life-long learner.

I grew up in a church that had a "lump" approach to disciple making; they "lumped" everybody together in the same growth environment. No one received guidance counseling or was advised on which learning environment best matched his stage of spiritual development. A new believer was treated the same as a mature believer. Everyone was lumped together according to chronological age rather than their spiritual stage of development.

The "lump" approach to disciple making places a person who does not know anything about the Bible in the same learning environment with a person who has read the Bible through many times. Or a person who knows nothing about the Trinity may be placed in the same environment as a person who has been taught doctrine for years. If academic institutions do not dare think of using the "lump" approach, why does the church?

As a person who is serious about making disciples, I challenge you to help each person you disciple find the appropriate environment and curriculum for their level of spiritual development. Give the person you disciple solid spiritual counsel. Do not lump them together with people who are at different stages of growth and development. We owe it to those we invest in to give them the best possible learning experience possible.

Impact Ministries is a resource you can use to find age- or "stage"-appropriate tools for disciple making. Impact has designed disciple-making curriculum for people who need basic growth, ministry training, and life-long learning. Check out the resources Impact has available at www.impactdiscipleship.com.

Day Sixty-Five:
"The Bible is Always Enough"

How does all this talk about "age- or stage-appropriate" disciple-making tools square up with how Jesus made disciples? Jesus did not use a course or curriculum when it came to making disciples. Jesus used the Old Testament Scriptures and His teachings to train His disciples. After all, Jesus was the "Word made flesh." Hebrews 1:1-2 says, *"In the past God spoke to our forefathers through the prophets at many times and in various ways, but in these last days He has spoken to us by His Son, whom He appointed heir of all things, and through whom He made the universe."* When God Himself is speaking, no other curriculum is necessary!

Jesus was obviously the Master Teacher. He was the perfect curriculum! Jesus knew exactly what His disciples needed, when they needed it, and He knew exactly how to give it to them. Jesus had no trouble whatsoever imparting truth to His disciples in the appropriate way. Being the *"Word made flesh"* (John 1:14), Jesus was in a unique position for disciple making that no one else will ever be in.

Our job as disciple makers is to take God's truth and communicate it to our disciples. The Bible will always be the curriculum we need for disciple making. We do not need any other source of truth in the disciple-making process. God's Word is enough.

Using tools that take us to the Scriptures is totally acceptable. In fact, that is exactly what happens when you hear a teacher or preacher communicate. A preacher is a tool God uses to bring people back to His truth. As long as the tool is connecting people to the truth, using the tool is a good thing. Substituting another source of truth is a bad thing. In fact, any source of truth other than the Bible is totally unacceptable.

I grew up going to a church where the Bible was taught, so I had a pretty good understanding of the Scriptures as a result of my church involvement and through my parents' influence. It wasn't until I went to seminary, however, that I studied systematic theology for a year where I was taught the Scriptures in a different format. During this class, some things I had heard my whole life took on a different meaning because I saw it from a new perspective. God's Word presented in a topical format opened up new levels of understanding for me. Discipleship tools can do the exact same thing.

A good discipleship curriculum should simply open up more of God's Word to you and help you dig even deeper into your Bible. If a discipleship course causes you to know more of God's truth, the tool has served you well. If a discipleship course does not build your knowledge of God's Word, you don't need it. The Bible ought to be the basis of every tool that claims to make disciples of Jesus.

I hope that even as you have read the chapters of this book, the truth of God has become more a part of your life. Every chapter has been tied to a verse of Scripture that teaches a principle of disciple making. We do not need to be tied to more opinions. We need to be tied to truth, and we need to teach those we disciple to be tied to the truth as well. May the Bible always be enough for you and the people you disciple.

Day Sixty-Six:
"Keep it Consistent"

If you've ever been to a track meet, you've probably seen relay races where a baton is passed between runners. The baton, or small round stick, is used by each team to make the connection in the race consistent for each team. You cannot throw or bounce the baton. It must be passed!

Once a track team begins a race, they do not change batons in the middle of the race; they use the same baton for each leg of the race. There is no way a team that stops to change batons could ever win a relay race. The principle of consistency in passing the baton is extremely important.

The other day a friend asked what I thought about a certain type of discipleship curriculum. I told him what I thought, and then asked if they were using it at his church. He said, "We are using several different types of disciple-making resources. We want to give people variety and choices in their resources."

I then asked, "How many of your groups have been successful at multiplying groups?"

He replied, "Reproducing groups has been one of our problems, and we have not been very successful at birthing new groups."

You are already ahead of me, right? You know exactly what I told my friend. I said, "You might be using too many batons."

"What?" he asked.

I replied, "You might be having trouble reproducing groups due to the fact that you have very little consistency in what is being taught."

I suggested he choose one training tool and stay consistent with that tool, which would make it much easier to monitor and motivate people to multiply additional groups. I also suggested that he might even try to create some structures by which people can work as a team in reproducing more discipleship groups. I'll have more on structures in the next lesson.

Using multiple resources for discipleship training is like changing batons during a relay. Relying on multiple resources is not wrong, but it isn't very effective. You will find it much harder to pass the baton and win the race if you keep changing the type of training you use. Consistency matters!

If you decide to use a tool for building disciples, I suggest you find one that leads people to the Bible, is based on the life of Christ, and is easy to pass on to others. My approach has been to make disciple making as "doable" for people as possible.

When you consider how busy people are these days, having an efficient and effective disciple-making process only makes sense. If the goal is to make disciples of "all nations," why make the process harder than it needs to be?

People can certainly create their own outlines and produce their own studies if they have the time. If not, they might find using a tool a good option to help them fulfill the Great Commission. After all, Jesus was not very specific on how we make disciples as long as we make disciples by teaching them to obey the things He has commanded (Matthew 28:20).

Hebrews 12:1-3 says, *"...let us run with perseverance the race marked out for us. Let us fix our eyes on Jesus, the author and perfecter of our faith, who for the joy set before Him endured the cross, scorning its shame, and sat down at the right hand of the throne of God. Consider Him who endured such opposition from sinful men, so that you will not grow weary and lose heart."*

Wouldn't it be awful to be in a track meet and have it recorded that you did not finish the race? I think even more tragic would be to live life and never multiply a single disciple of Jesus Christ. If having a consistent tool for multiplying disciples will help me prosper in making disciples, then by all means let me "keep it consistent"!

Day Sixty-Seven:
"Maintain Structure"

We live in a world with structure. Schools have semester or quarter systems. Companies have work shifts. Governments have sessions. Sports teams have seasons. Structure is valuable because organization and systems help us accomplish certain tasks. Can you imagine a school with no structure? Teaching students in an environment where there was no beginning point and ending point would be extremely hard. Evaluating and advancing students would be almost impossible if there was no system for testing and promotion. If everyone did "self-study," there would be no need for a school. Structure wouldn't be necessary.

Disciple making works best with a certain amount of structure and is more effective when there is some type of system in place to help people grow. Certainly growth is the result of the Holy Spirit working in our lives, but the Holy Spirit uses our structures and systems to make growth happen. Paul even tells us in 1 Corinthians 14:33, *"For God is not a God of disorder but of peace."* Obviously, God uses order.

I have seen a fair share of discipleship groups that change meeting times, regularly skip weekly meetings, and change the day they meet each week. Sometimes, with strong leadership and commitment, those types of groups are successful, but my experience has shown me that most of the time they are not.

Over the years, I have been reasonably consistent in working out with weights three to five times a week. When I work out at a set time on set days, I tend to have better results than when I mix up my workout days and times. The structure plays a big part in my effectiveness for physical growth. As with weight lifting, the role of structure in our spiritual growth is just as important.

In the very early accounts of the growth of the church in the book of Acts, we see that structure played a big part in the growth of the church and individuals. They met together in set places and at set times for certain activities. The Holy Spirit used their devotion to *"teaching, fellowship, the breaking of bread and prayer"* (Acts 2:42) to produce tremendous spiritual fruit in their lives. Read the second chapter of the book of Acts to learn more.

So why not try it? Invite a small group of potential disciples to meet with you at a set place on a set day at a set time for a set number of weeks and with a set plan. When those individuals are ready to multiply more disciples, invite them to start their groups in the same way. If you follow this structure and system, it will not take long until you have a movement of disciple making. Maybe that movement will grow over time and impact people you don't even know in places you will never go. Amazing what a little structure can do, isn't it?

God is a God of order. You see order in everything God does. Why wouldn't He use order in the way we go about making disciples? I encourage you to have just enough order in the disciple-making process for the Holy Spirit to work, but not so much order that the Holy Spirit is quenched. He will help you find the balance if you simply ask. Be committed to a structured environment!

Day Sixty-Eight:
"Ambassador of the Brand"

I have a very good friend who works for a fast-food organization that is famous for "inventing the chicken sandwich, but not the chicken." My buddy is a loyal employee who describes himself as being an "ambassador of the brand." He has obviously heard someone communicate the importance of being a champion for the product they are selling. In all honesty, I would have to say that my friend is a great ambassador for his company. He truly represents what the company is about. He believes in their mission, and he carries out his role in a professional way. If anybody is out championing the cause of this company, it is this man.

My friend is also another kind of ambassador. He is not only a champion of his company; he is also a champion of the Great Commandment and Great Commission. You could say he is a champion of disciple making! He truly represents what Jesus Christ is all about. He believes in Christ's mission and carries out his role as a disciple maker in a faithful way. If anybody is out championing disciple making, it is this man.

Now that you are on day sixty-eight, I'm sure you realize I believe every disciple ought to be an ambassador of the brand! In other words, each disciple of Jesus Christ should be a champion of disciple making.

Observing what people champion with their lives can be very interesting. I see people who are champions of worship. I see people who are champions of evangelism. I see people who are champions for leadership. I see people who are champions for the Scriptures. I see people who are champions for social action. I see people who are champions for just about everything you can think of in ministry. They passionately believe in a cause, and they pursue it with great fervor. They "buy in," so to speak.

My concern is, how can any disciple of Jesus Christ *not* be bought-in to disciple making? How can a disciple of Jesus not champion the very thing Jesus did? How can a disciple of Jesus not be an ambassador of making more disciples? How can a fast-food company, in many ways, be more successful than the church of Jesus Christ? I say that only in the context of the church's ability to create a movement of multiplying disciples who are champions of disciple making. I am not convinced that the church is equipping people to do what Jesus has called us to do. In order to get back to being ambassadors of the brand, I think we need to remember a few things.

First, we must remember that ambassadors are what they represent. An ambassador from the United States needs to be a citizen of the United States of America. Championing something that is not true of you is almost impossible. You will not champion disciple making if you are not being and building disciples of Christ.

Secondly, we must remember that ambassadors are authorized by their country as representatives to others of what their nation believes. An ambassador of the United States would always support democracy. You would never find a U.S. Ambassador supporting communism. In Matthew 28:18 Jesus says, *"All authority in heaven and on earth has been given to Me."* Jesus then authorized His disciples to make more disciples. We champion disciple making when we live up to the authority given to us.

An ambassador of a chicken company might champion the cause by encouraging people to "eat more chicken." An ambassador of Jesus Christ would champion the cause of Christ by encouraging people to "make more disciples." Are you an ambassador of the brand? Are you championing disciple making?

Day Sixty-Nine:
"The Day I Became a Champion"

I remember it well: Thursday, April 29th, 1999. I was attending a disciple-making conference at a retreat center in North Carolina. Little did I know God was going to make this event a defining moment in my life.

I was attending with several other staff members from the church where I serve as Senior Pastor. It was a particularly difficult time for me and for the church. We seemed to have hit a wall in our growth. At the same time, we had several key families bailing out, and I was experiencing a serious turmoil.

While I was attending the Thursday night session of the conference, God spoke to me in a powerful way. The speaker began to share the vision God had given him for the ministry he was leading. He shared many of the highs and lows that came with watching this vision become more of a reality. I remember thinking that "his" vision wasn't really "his" vision but *God's* vision. This leader was simply carrying out God's vision to reach all nations by making disciples.

The speaker concluded his message by challenging the leaders in the room to discover God's vision for their ministry. Then it hit me like a ton of bricks: God's vision was to be my vision. There was no need to discover a new vision. I simply needed to discover how God wanted me to join Him to fulfill His vision.

When the meeting concluded, one of the staff guys asked me if I wanted to go with everyone else for some ice cream. Rarely do I ever turn down ice cream, but this was one of those times. I went straight to my room, took out my Bible and started to write. Here are the exact words I wrote in the back of my Bible that evening.

There are 3 things I know for certain God has called me to do.

These are my calling, my purpose, my vision and mission. As sure as I know God saved me, and Val was the woman I was meant to marry, I know God has called me to …

1 – Live as an authentic disciple to the best of my ability.

2 – Lead a local church to make disciples who make disciples.

3 – Help other churches learn how to be disciple-making churches.

I believe this is my life's calling, and He will send the people, resources, places, and opportunities to enable me to accomplish this calling.

Thursday, April 29th, 1999 was the day I became a champion of the disciple-making lifestyle. I became an ambassador of the brand! Yes, I will do plenty of other things in ministry, but you will always find me making disciples. I have no other choice. I have submitted my life to the vision of Jesus Christ. Disciple making is not my vision but God's. I may champion many different causes in my life, but I must always champion the cause of making disciples of all nations.

I pray you have become a champion of disciple making and have submitted to Christ's vision as well. I hope you have had your own defining moment in life. If not, I hope today is the day. I pray His vision will become your vision!

Day Seventy:
"Leaders are Readers"

I'm sure you've heard the phrase, "Leaders are readers." I believe that statement is true, but I'd like to add to it: "Disciple-making leaders are readers of disciple making."

As someone who feels called to champion disciple making, I am sure you will want to read as much as you can on the topic. If that is the case, I have good news and bad news for you. The good news is that there have been some really great books written on the subject of disciple making. In the remainder of this lesson I will give you the names of some books and authors that are "must reads" for every serious disciple maker. The bad news is that those great books are few and far between. If you start looking for books on disciple making, you will be surprised how few there are on this topic and how rarely new books on disciple making are published. One would think there would be an abundance of books on the very thing Christ came to do.

On the contrary, there is no surplus of books on disciple making. There have been some great books written on the subject, and hopefully you can still find them in the bookstores. Let me start with a couple of classic works. Every serious disciple maker needs to read <u>The Master Plan of Evangelism</u> by Robert Coleman and <u>The Lost Art of Disciple Making</u> by Leroy Eims. These two books are like primers for anyone who wants to grow in their knowledge of how to make disciples of Jesus Christ.

Bill Hull wrote one of the best series of books on disciple making I have ever read. I would strongly recommend every disciple maker read all three — <u>The Disciple Making Church</u>, <u>Jesus Christ Disciple Maker</u>, and <u>The Disciple Making Pastor</u>. These books give great insight into the practical steps Jesus took in building a disciple-making movement.

I would also recommend several books for anyone who wants to gain a solid Christology as a foundation for disciple making. Dann Spader and Gary Mays wrote a great book called <u>Growing a Healthy Church</u>. Carl Wilson wrote a very scholarly work on disciple making titled <u>With Christ in the School of Disciple Building</u>. In addition, a book called <u>Personal Disciple Making</u> written by Chris Adsit gives a great breakdown of various stages of spiritual development. <u>Transforming</u>

Discipleship written by Greg Ogden is one of the newer books filled with great biblical truths of Christ's approach to disciple making. A book by Ron Lee Davis titled Mentoring — The Strategy of the Master is another great book to read on the disciple-making process.

I have read two books that I highly recommend that might be difficult to find these days. One is called Multiplying Disciples by Waylon Moore and the other is a study course written by Charles Swindoll called Discipleship … Ministry Up Close and Personal. If you can get your hands on these books, you will have a small treasure of information.

The study course written by Avery Willis called MasterLife is one of the best disciple-making study courses available. The book version is a great read as well. Finally, one of the most recent publications on disciple making is The Great Omission by Dallas Willard. This book is a compilation of writings on disciple making by Mr. Willard.

In 2 Timothy 4:13 Paul says, *"When you come, bring the cloak that I left with Carpus at Troas, and my scrolls, especially the parchments."* Paul was obviously a reader and a great leader. Never forget, leaders are readers. Keep reading!

Day Seventy-One:
"Good Enough for Jesus, Good Enough for Me"

Our local newspaper has a section titled "The Vent" where people write in and tell what is aggravating them. Instead of venting to our local paper, I am venting my frustrations here more than I am informing or inspiring anyone to a lifestyle of disciple making. I placed this lesson near the end of the book so hopefully by now you would be just as frustrated as I am by what I am about to share.

I have had conversations with and heard people talk about the need to replace the words "discipleship, disciple, and disciple making" with more relevant terminology. Many people are choosing to replace these timeless biblical words with more modern-day phrases. They feel it is more beneficial to use words like "mentoring, coaching, and partnering" to relate to today's culture.

I think I'm fairly forward thinking when it comes to ministry that is relating to the culture. I've even been accused of bringing Satan into the church because we started singing contemporary praise and worship songs. All we are trying to do is relate to the culture we are trying to reach with a different musical sound. I have communicated our culturally relevant philosophy many times by using the statement, "We will always be willing to change our methods, but we will never be willing to change the message!"

So what about those who want to change the vocabulary? I guess that's okay as long as it doesn't change the message. I personally may never be able to see Jesus saying, "Go make mentors or coaches of all nations," but if the end result is the same, why argue over terminology?

The main goal of disciple making is to help people become fully trained Christ followers. What those people are called doesn't really matter. In fact, Christ followers were not even called Christians until several years after Jesus ascended back to heaven. Acts 11:26 says, *"... The disciples were called Christians first at Antioch."*

I guess you can call me "old school" or a "has been," but I'm sticking with the phrase "disciple making." It was good enough for Jesus; it will be good enough for me. In fact, I'm sticking with the word "discipleship" because there are just some things I think should stand out from culture.

You can go to the gym and hear people referred to as "fitness coaches," but you never hear anyone being referred to as a "fitness discipler." In the academic setting you will hear people called "academic mentors," but never will you hear the phrase "academic discipler." I guess my point is that some words are just set apart from the culture. I think being called a "disciple" of Jesus Christ is one of those words.

Maybe I am splitting hairs or making much to-do about nothing. I'll give you that. If you want to make "mentors of all nations," I can live with that as long as they are mentors of Jesus Christ. I just want you to know I am sticking with making "disciples of all nations," and I thank you for reading my vent.

Day Seventy-Two:
"Seasons of Disciple Making"

Ecclesiastes 3:1 says, *"There is a time for everything, and a season for every activity under heaven..."* That includes a time and season for making disciples. Everyone goes through different seasons in life. Like the seasons of the year, our lives change, and we find ourselves facing different circumstances. Throughout the years I have seen some very committed disciple makers face the seasons of life.

One of the most faithful disciple makers I know faced a tough season of life when his young daughter passed away. As this little girl battled hard to fight the cancer in her body, her father faced a tremendously difficult season in his own life. After his little girl passed away, my friend needed to go through a season of healing. He will never get over his daughter's death, but he has gotten on with his life. Her dying has made him even more resolved to make disciples. He knows this is the best way for him to impact eternity.

A man I spent several years investing in as a disciple had a huge moral failure in his life. This moral train wreck side-tracked his disciple-making efforts for a number of years. Once my friend came clean with his sin, he underwent several years of recovery and counseling to break the bonds of sin that had gripped his life. My friend will always be in recovery, but he is back in the disciple-making game. A serious moral failure does not exempt us from obeying the Great Commission. In fact, my buddy approaches his investment in others in a totally different way than before. He has much more grace and humility as he helps others grow as disciples of Christ. By the way, my buddy not only leads a discipleship group, he also leads a recovery group. He has turned a very negative in his life into a positive.

I know a gal who isn't able to invest in disciples the way she would like because she has a daughter with some very serious disabilities. Her little girl needs her attention twenty-four/seven. She is in a season of life that makes any kind of commitment very hard to keep. This lady is very committed to making disciples, but it does not happen in the conventional manner.

I know of people who face seasons of life where their schedule makes it difficult to make disciples. A young stay-at-home mom has a very different schedule from a working mom with school-age children. A busy executive who travels three to four days a week has a very different schedule than a man who is retired. We all face seasons of life when our schedules make the priority of disciple making either easy or difficult.

I believe the main goal of disciple making is longevity. I know there will be times and seasons in my life when I am investing in people and times when I am not. The short seasons are not as important to me as the long haul. Needing to take a break from discipling people is not a big issue. Never having the priority in your life is a huge issue!

One priority I have seen with disciple makers is that they make time for making disciples. To spend a couple of years teaching someone to be a Christ follower does not simply happen. It is the result of a very intentional commitment of time. When you come to the end of your life, I hope you can look back and see that you have made a faithful investment in the lives of your children and a few individuals you helped learn to walk as Jesus did.

Day Seventy-Three:
"Any Place, Any Time"

I see three men in a fast-food restaurant at 6:00 on Friday mornings doing discipleship. I see four women in a popular coffee shop at 7:30 on a Thursday night working through their discipleship lesson. I hear about four men who meet on Saturday mornings around a kitchen table to hold each other accountable as a part of their discipleship relationship. I sit in a circle of six men on a Sunday afternoon at 4:00 and listen to them quote Scripture as a part of our discipleship time together. I see a handful of students meeting with their Student Pastor in his office on Sunday mornings for discipleship. I see and hear about these disciple-making environments and am reminded that disciple making can take place in any place and at any time.

I guess if you asked me, "Where is the ideal place to make disciples," I would say, "The church." I'm not necessarily saying that it needs to happen in the church building; I am simply saying that it ought to happen in the church context. I mean, even Paul spent time *"with the disciples in Damascus"* after he was saved according to Acts 9:19. In New Testament times disciple making taking place within the Body of Christ seemed logical.

Hopefully you are involved in a church that has created environments where discipleship can take place. Discipleship that happens in the context of biblical community is a very rich experience. If, however, you are in a church that has no environment for discipleship, I suggest you make disciples anyway. You will answer to God for what you did with the Great Commission regardless of what your church did.

If you are not in a church that is promoting a disciple-making environment, I suggest you look around you for opportunities to invest in potential disciples. You may know people in your neighborhood you can invite to join you in discipleship. You may have friends you work with or go to school with who have a desire to grow deeper in Christ. I once invited a man I coached Little League with to join me once a week for a basic discipleship course. There is no end to the possibilities of people the Lord would have you disciple.

I guess if you asked, "When is the ideal time to make disciples," I would say, "Any time is the right time." Most of us do not have the luxury of spending as much time with our disciples as Jesus spent with the first disciples. We only have a certain number of hours each week we can use to invest in those we disciple. Any time you can get a few people to commit to meeting together on a regular basis is an acceptable time to do discipleship. I actually believe the more options we have for meeting together the better. In today's world, people work so many different shifts and schedules, it makes sense to have discipleship groups meeting at many different times.

I still believe the local church is the best place to match people up in discipleship environments. If the church can be the organizational structure to help people find a discipleship environment, our chances of success are increased.

One of the beautiful things about disciple making is the flexibility of when you can meet and where you can meet. If I didn't know better, I would think God created it that way just so we would have fewer excuses for not being obedient. So what is your excuse?

Day Seventy-Four:
"Any One, Any How"

Disciple making may be able to take place in any place at any time, but the process is not intended to be led by any person in any way possible. A discipleship group needs to be led by a person who is qualified. Even Jesus did not send out His disciples until they had first been discipled. Here is the key. Does the person who wants to lead demonstrate the qualities that are expected of a leader in this capacity?

Some expectations are obvious. A non-believer should not be leading a discipleship group. Some qualifications, however, are not so obvious. Should a person who is not giving to the church be leading others in discipleship? Would we agree that a person who is not a church member is not qualified to lead a discipleship group? Can a person who is not sharing his or her faith be leading a discipleship group? Should a person who is in marriage counseling with his or her spouse be in charge of helping others grow spiritually?

I think there are some important issues we need to sort out as we think about the qualifications of leadership. First, let's agree that leadership does have qualifications. When leaders were chosen in the early church notice the qualifications, *"Brothers, choose seven men from among you who are known to be full of the Spirit and wisdom"* (Acts 6:3). Obviously, selection was based on qualifications. A second observation is that there needs to be certain "basic" qualifications. By basic qualifications I suggest leaders ought to be modeling what they are teaching. Being a believer is a basic qualification. Being a church member is a basic qualification. I could go on and on, but the basic qualifications are the characteristics of Christ. If identity, community, maturity, and ministry do not exist in a leader's life, he or she is not modeling what they are asking a Christ follower to become. Finally, we should all be able to agree that the qualification for leadership is progress, not perfection. Even Jesus did not send out perfect leaders. Jesus did send out leaders who were making progress!

Leading a discipleship group is not a job that just anyone can do. There are qualifications that are prerequisites for leadership.

A discipleship group needs to be led by a qualified leader, and it needs to be led in a God-honoring way. I hate to say it, but I have heard too many cases of discipleship gone bad. I have heard too many stories of people abusing their leadership in a disciple-making relationship. I have heard stories of people who cause doctrinal damage in those they disciple. I have heard horror tales of those who have influenced their disciples into immoral activity. I have known disciple leaders who have created disunity in the church rather than promote unity. I have seen discipleship leaders who have been unethical and unbiblical in their dealings with others. I will spare you the gory details, but over the years, I have seen some disciple leaders lead in the wrong direction.

I hope by now you have drawn a simple yet powerful conclusion. God-qualified leaders create God-honoring groups! The best way to develop a discipleship group that honors God is to be a leader qualified by God. I hope you are becoming that kind of leader, and I hope you are building those kinds of leaders. Discipleship is not just for anyone to be done any way they choose.

Day Seventy-Five:
"The Disciple-Making Pocketbook"

I love the story of the man who was being baptized and accidentally left his wallet in his pocket. The pastor apologized to him but he said, "Oh no pastor, I'm giving Him everything—money and all."

Even Jesus told us that we can never separate our heart from our money. In Matthew 6:21 Jesus said, *"For where your treasure is, there your heart will be also."* Jesus pulls no punches about the connection between our stuff and what we love the most. You can fake prayer, Bible reading, and worship, but you cannot fake giving.

I've tried to show you throughout this book that God's heart beats for disciple making. Anything God's heart beats for our heart ought to beat for as well. If our treasure indicates where our heart is, then our pocketbooks ought to support disciple making. In other words, anyone who is devoted to disciple making will demonstrate it in their giving.

Obviously, the clearest expression of giving toward disciple making is through the ministry of your local church. Hopefully your church prioritizes the Great Commission and, therefore, is a great place for you to give of your resources. The church where I am a member is staunchly committed to the disciple-making process, and I know my offering is going toward the fulfillment of the Great Commission.

One of the reasons I stress the connection between giving and disciple making is because I am often asked by people where they should donate after giving to their local church. I know many people give to their church and are still able to give over and above to other ministries. Of all the ministry opportunities available, I think it is important to ask which option is the best use of your money.

I know I could give to a number of different ministries, but I believe I need to give my resources to disciple-making ministries, thereby placing my funds in a ministry that has a multiplying effect. I know my money honors God when it is given to a ministry that will have a continual investment. If I give a dollar to multiplication, that dollar lives on in many generations of disciples. What better way to honor God with my resources? When my church prioritizes the multiplication of disciples, I am giving my resources to a cause that will yield eternal dividends. I cannot go wrong when I have a disciple-making pocketbook.

Over the years, I have known several people who have given faithfully to their local church and have also supported disciple making with sacrificial gifts. Impact Ministries has been one of those to benefit from such gifts. As Impact Ministries comes alongside the local church to make disciples, it becomes a stewardship win-win.

I share this lesson with you not to ask for money, but simply to remind you of the importance of having your money match up with your heart. Jesus tells disciple makers, *"...I am with you always, to the very end of the age"* (Matthew 28:20). That being the case, I want my money to clearly demonstrate my priorities. Disciple making is my priority, and I want my wallet to prove it.

How about you?

Day Seventy-Six:
"From Newnan to Social Circle"

On Day Six I told you the story of how God used Tim to help start a movement of multiplying disciples in LaGrange, Georgia, a small town not far from where I live. Today I want to share with you a similar story that has led to a movement of multiplication about an hour-and-a-half drive north of LaGrange.

Seven years ago a small church in Social Circle had a series of revival services where the speaker issued a challenge to the men of the church. He challenged 10% of them to gather together to pray once a week. About two dozen men responded to the challenge and began to meet once a week for prayer. Over time the number of men began to drop from a couple dozen men to a group of four men who have met each week for a number of years to pray.

As a result of prayer, the men sensed God leading them to reach out to other men in their community. They wanted to challenge men to be true disciples of Jesus Christ. They wanted to challenge the men in their churches and in their community to be the spiritual leaders God intended them to be.

These four men decided to have a gathering and challenge as many men as they could to attend. They found a lodge on a ranch where they could have this gathering and cooked up a mess of barbeque to feed everyone. They wanted someone to speak to the men at this gathering on the importance of being a disciple of Christ. One of the men in the group had been given a copy of an Impact Discipleship course, so he decided to contact me about speaking at this event.

I was honored to be able to speak to this group and sensed God was up to something as I heard them share their story. As I stood before this group of about forty men, I felt God was doing something, and I was simply being allowed to join Him where He was working. The evening went very well. Everyone seemed to enjoy the fellowship and appeared to be engaged in the event. I even sensed a real receptiveness to the message and received some very positive feedback from my challenge to be and build disciples of Jesus Christ.

About a week after the gathering I received an e-mail message from one of the men who organized the event. He informed me that their group was now so large that they have had to divide into two groups. I wonder if another movement of multiplying disciples has begun. I wonder how many lives can be touched as a result of the faithfulness of these men to reach out. I can't wait to see how God might use this group of men to radically impact their community for Christ.

When I hear stories of movements of multiplying disciples in places like Newnan, LaGrange, and Social Circle, I can't help but think of the way the Gospel spread in the New Testament days. In Acts 11:21 the Scripture says, *"The Lord's hand was with them, and a great number of people believed and turned to the Lord."* The believers in Acts were experiencing God! His hand was with them. As I understand the words of Jesus, He has promised His hand will be on us as well. In Matthew 28:19-20 Jesus promises to be with us if we live according to His mission. Why would we dare miss that promise?

Day Seventy-Seven:
"Make Disciples—Not!"

Here it is…a sure-fire plan for how <u>not</u> to make a multiplying disciple of Christ:

First, make a big deal about a person's spiritual birth, but don't say anything about spiritual growth. If possible, convince people to be saved and satisfied. Now that they know they are headed to heaven when they die, they won't have to worry about any other spiritual development. I have known people who have worn spiritual "diapers" for years and never matured into a fully trained disciple of Christ.

Second, get them so busy doing church stuff they don't have time to learn how to be a disciple. Sometimes believers can be involved in so much activity yet have no true productivity for the Kingdom. Someone said, "If Satan cannot make you bad, he will make you busy." I have known many people who are so busy in their church they have no time for making disciples.

Third, focus so much on giving people information without calling for application. People can often be overloaded with so much knowledge that they never apply any of it. I agree with one assessment, "This generation of believers is one of the best educated in history." I have known people who jump from one Bible study to the next and never stop to make a disciple. I don't think Jesus said, "Go make Bible students of all nations." Disciples need to know the Bible, but they also need to do what the Bible says to do.

Fourth, keep people in the context of large groups and never let them connect to a small group where life-on-life transformation takes place. People commonly like to sit and soak in the large crowd. Once they soak for awhile, they will begin to sour. I have know many people who have stayed in the comfort of the large group and never experienced the transforming power of a small group of disciples.

Fifth, do everything you can for the new believer and never give him a chance to figure things out on his own. Growth always requires resistance. If you keep a disciple from stretching his or her spiritual wings, he might never learn to fly. I have known many people who have been safeguarded and spoon-fed their entire spiritual lives and never reached their potential for Christ.

Sixth, never give a person the chance to lead another person in a discipleship experience. Keep the concept of "I do with you, now you go do with another" far from their thinking. If you give a person an opportunity to experience leading another person in spiritual growth, he or she might get excited about it and continue doing so for a lifetime. I know people who have never made a disciple because they were never given the opportunity to lead someone in that process.

Are you starting to get the point? If we are not intentional about the process of making disciples, we will unintentionally prevent people from making disciples. So often we are doing so many good things that we miss doing the best thing. Don't miss out on the thrill of leading people to the place where they are reproducing their faith in Christ in another.

Remember Ephesians 5:1, *"Be imitators of God, therefore, as dearly loved children..."* When you imitate God, you will make disciples—Yes!

Day Seventy-Eight:
"Where Do Disciples Come From?"

Every parent is asked the dreaded question, "Where do babies come from?" Sooner or later parents have to muster up the courage to explain the process of reproduction to their child. The words might seem awkward and the explanation might be difficult to communicate, but you know all parents have the responsibility of teaching their child where babies come from.

As Christians, we ought to wrestle with the question, "Where do disciples come from?" Sooner or later, every believer in Jesus Christ needs to understand the process of spiritual reproduction. Communicating this concept can be difficult if the process has never been demonstrated. If the responsibility for training disciples to make more disciples is neglected, the value of reproducing disciples will be forgotten.

If **"personal multiplication"** is not taught to the next generation of believers, what will happen? Will the personal be replaced with the programmatic? A very real danger exists in this generation of believers who might begin to think that disciple making is the result of a program, rather than the result of intentional relationships.

What happens if multiplication is replaced with addition? Another danger is that this generation of believers will start to accept the growth of Christianity by addition rather than multiplication.

The enemy would certainly want us to forget where disciples come from, wouldn't he? The enemy would love to convince us that being a personal multiplier of disciples of Jesus Christ is not really the reason we exist. If the enemy can get us distracted with many things, we can lose sight of the single most important thing we can be about on planet earth — making disciples!

In Genesis 1:28, God told Adam and Eve to *"be fruitful and multiply, and fill the earth, and subdue it"* (NASB). In Genesis 9:1, God told Noah to *"be fruitful and multiply, and fill the earth"* (NASB). In John 15:8 Jesus tells His disciples *"bear much fruit, showing yourselves to be My disciples."* God is much more concerned with the process of multiplication than we are.

Don't you find it interesting that God did not command us to "worship," "learn," or "work"? God commanded us to "multiply"! Yes, God wants us to worship Him and learn more about Him. Yes, God wants us to serve Him, but God's ultimate agenda is to see every person come into a saving and growing relationship with Himself. We demonstrate we are Christ's disciples when we bear much fruit.

Do you know where disciples come from? Are you taking personal responsibility for the value of making disciples who make more disciples? Is "personal multiplication" a characteristic of your life? Do not let the priority of reproducing disciples get lost on your watch. Do not let the enemy distract you from the right focus. Make disciples! Be fruitful and multiply the life of Jesus Christ in as many people as possible in the time you have left.

Day Seventy-Nine:
"How Deep is Deep Enough?"

I recently asked a man if his college-age son was still attending our church. He informed me that his son was attending another church at times because he "wanted to go deeper." I wanted to ask the man if his son needed to go deeper because he had already applied everything he knew. I certainly understand the need to go deeper. I desire to go deeper in my knowledge of God; however, I also want to go deeper in my *application* of the knowledge of God.

I find it hard to accept the "I want to go deeper" claim when most people are not applying what they already know. Many people who claim the need to go deeper are not tithing, not sharing their faith, not serving, not living in personal holiness, not living in right relationships, and not multiplying disciples. At what point does the "I want to go deeper" claim simply become an excuse for not being obedient to what one already knows?

My hunch is that many who claim the need to go deeper are more interested in "different" than they are "depth." I believe the man's son mentioned above really wants to hear something different more than he wants to hear something deeper. I say that because I know firsthand that this individual is not yet applying what he already knows.

I have been a Christ follower for almost fifty years. I have graduated from seminary and have been in ministry for over twenty-five years. I have logged countless hours of study and listened to more messages than you can imagine. I consider myself to have gone deeper in my knowledge of Christ's life than I ever imagined.

I might simply be a slow learner, but I must confess that I am educated well above my level of obedience. Daily I find myself still trying to obey the most basic of spiritual truths. My prayer life is still not what it needs to be. My Bible study is not where I'd like it to be. I still struggle to share my faith the way I want to. I give in to temptation at times when I know better. I neglect managing my time and temple the way I know God wants me to. I don't always treat people the way I know God would want me to. Going deeper is obviously not my problem! Obeying what I already know to be true is my problem.

I will continue to grow in my understanding of God and His Word. That pursuit is not optional for me. I am a life-long learner. I will, however, never use the claim for going deeper as an excuse for not doing what I already know I ought to be doing.

One of the most basic truths of Scripture is the command Jesus gave us to *"make disciples of all nations."* How are you doing with that command? Do you just need something a little heavier? Do those words not stimulate you enough? Are you just picking and choosing the commands you want to obey? Go as deep in the things of God as you can go, but never let depth be a substitute for obedience!

Day Eighty:
"Five Loaves and Two Fish"

Mark 6:41-42 says, *"Taking the five loaves and the two fish and looking up to heaven, He gave thanks and broke the loaves. Then He gave them to His disciples to set before the people. He also divided the two fish among them all. They all ate and were satisfied."* Every time I read that story I am reminded that Christ has the power to take the little bit I have and multiply it in order to feed a multitude.

The other day I was talking to a friend who gave a challenge to a group of men in his church to be disciples of Jesus Christ. He even had a sign-up sheet for anyone who might be interested in becoming a part of a discipleship group. To say my friend was surprised when over thirty men signed up is an understatement.

My buddy was experiencing some major anxiety when he called me to share the results of his challenge. He didn't know what to do with the thirty guys he had just recruited for an Impact Discipleship group. He was currently taking four men through the Impact process and now he had more guys to feed than he had loaves and fish to offer.

With a few suggestions I assured my disciple-making brother that God was big enough to handle his situation. If he simply gave the little he had to God, a miracle could be in the making. God can take the sincere efforts of my friend, bless his commitment to make disciples, raise up qualified leaders, and get hungry men into discipleship groups.

God can multiply our small handful of resources today just as He did two thousand years ago. In reflecting over the dilemma my friend faces with the men in his church, I am reminded of several important disciple-making principles.

First, circumstances do not have to be perfect before we are willing to make disciples. If we wait until we have enough resources to feed five thousand, we might never feed anybody. Give God what you have, where you are, and let Him take care of the rest.

Secondly, God has already blessed disciple making so we know He will take care of the results. Making disciples is not something you have to pray about doing. God has already made it perfectly clear that He wants us to be making disciples of all nations. You already have His blessing; what God wants is your obedience. So often we don't give God what we have because we have forgotten He gave it to us in the first place.

Finally, making a disciple is your chance to take part in a miracle. Just think. If God uses you to impact thousands of lives because you were willing to invest in a handful of people, it will be an obvious miracle. Your ability to influence countless people for Christ through disciple making will bring God glory and be a miraculous event.

I hope this lesson encourages you to give God what He has given you. Don't question whether you have what it takes to make a disciple. Just give God what you have and trust Him with the outcome. You might just be surprised how far He can take the little handful you have to offer.

Day Eighty-One:
"Who is Your Copilot?"

I was listening to a friend tell a story about the time a pilot handed him the controls of a small airplane in the middle of his flight. That may not sound like anything big to you, but it was major news to me. There are two things you need to understand about my buddy's admission. First, he does not have a pilot's license, nor does he know how to fly a plane. Secondly, I was on that plane along with his wife and my wife when my "wannabe" pilot friend took the controls for a brief moment in time.

While my friend sat in the copilot seat, the pilot took his hands off the controls for just a minute or two. No one could tell, but the plane dropped about 100 feet while my buddy was in control. Before things got out of hand, the real pilot regained control of the airplane and gave us a safe flight to our destination.

This story serves as a great illustration of the lessons I have learned about making disciples over the years. Let me share a few of those principles with you.

A person must be trained before being responsible. The difference between my friend and the pilot of our plane was the amount of training they had been given. The pilot had logged hundreds of hours in the cockpit while my buddy had zero hours logged. The hours of training the pilot had received gave him the right to have responsibility for flying that plane. I know a bunch of church leaders who have been given responsibility without being trained. That is why Jesus said, *"Make disciples."*

A part of being trained is having someone else alongside you. When the pilot of our plane was training to fly, he had a more experienced pilot alongside him just like my friend did. My friend wasn't in training, but even he was able to try something without fear of failure because the pilot was sitting right beside him. When Jesus trained His disciples, He was right there alongside them. That didn't mean they were exempt from problems; it simply meant He would be there when they needed Him. Jesus is still there for us today. He sent His Holy Spirit to empower us to do the task of making disciples. We have the Master disciple maker right beside us.

The goal of every pilot is to fly solo. I don't think there has ever been a person who learned to fly so they could stay in the copilot seat. Every flight student I have ever known had one goal in mind—flying solo.

Flying airplanes and making disciples are very similar. Christ didn't tell us to make disciples so that we could spend the rest of our lives watching everybody else make disciples. Christ wants us to fly solo. God's plan is for you to personally experience the process of leading someone to be a disciple. How are you doing in fulfilling that plan?

The Psalmist says in Psalm 86:11, *"Teach me Your way, O Lord, and I will walk in Your truth; give me an undivided heart, that I may fear Your name."*

Good pilots have been trained. Someone has taken the time to teach them how to fly a plane to the best of their ability, given the circumstances. Being a disciple maker requires training. If you are willing to be taught, God will take you to new heights.

Day Eighty-Two:
"Newnan to Hood River, via Steamboat"

One of the most exciting things in life is being surprised by God. I recently experienced another one of God's little surprises. Let me tell you what happened.

I live a few miles south of Atlanta, Georgia … in the Deep South. I was recently invited to teach at a men's retreat in a place called Hood River, Oregon … in the far northwest. Actually, the retreat was a few hours' drive outside of the city. In other words, I was in a remote city far, far away from Newnan, Georgia!

The retreat was incredible. God did a neat work in the hearts of the men present, and many of them left that weekend with a vision and passion for living lives of multiplying more disciples of Christ. I was honored to be able to be a part of what God was doing in that place.

As the retreat progressed, I discovered another amazing thing about how God works. I asked the director of the retreat, Cory, how he came to contact me as a potential retreat speaker. Cory told me about a man named John who lives in Steamboat Springs, Colorado, during the winter and in the Hood River, Oregon, area with his family during the summer. While John was in Hood River one summer, he introduced Impact Discipleship to the church he attends there. Many of the men who were attending our retreat had come from that same church, where they had been introduced to Impact. As a result of this sequence of events, they asked me to teach at the retreat.

The story actually began several years ago when Cindy, a gal in my church, introduced me to her brother Kevin. Kevin became pastor of a church in Steamboat Springs, Colorado. He invited me to come to his church and do some training in disciple making. I spent a few days in his church, and several small discipleship groups started in Steamboat as a result of our time together.

Over the years, those Impact Discipleship groups in Steamboat have spread to other churches in that area. From one of those churches, a man named John took the Impact Discipleship program to Hood River, Oregon, where he spends his summers.

John obviously understands what Jesus meant when He said, *"Go and make disciples of all nations."* I'm sure Jesus included Steamboat and Hood River in *"all nations"*!

Do you see what I mean by "God's surprises"? I could not have manufactured this course of events if my life depended on it. God is the One who orchestrated these relationships so that He could accomplish His purposes in the world. As always, all God was looking for was willing vessels. A gal named Cindy, a man named Kevin, a guy named John, a man named Cory, and a guy named Ken are all simply tools in the hands of the Master disciple maker.

In Numbers 14:21 the Bible says, *"...but indeed, as I live, all the earth will be filled with the glory of the Lord"* (NASB). I believe it. God has proven to me that the earth is filled with His glory. I've even seen it from one coast to the other. What a great surprise to be around when God reveals a little bit of His glory.

Day Eighty-Three:
"Unlikely Disciples"

Which of these two would you pick as the most likely candidate to make a disciple? The first choice is a young man who just graduated from seminary. He has been a Christian since high school and is a very sharp young man. He is looking for a ministry position on a church staff and is very committed to being in an innovative style of ministry that is reaching today's generation.

Your second choice is a man in his early seventies. He has been a Christian longer than the other candidate has been alive. Many years ago he sang in a gospel quartet, and he loves the sound of the old hymns. This gentleman has been a Sunday school teacher for years and feels very much at home in a traditional style church service.

I can't trick you, can I? You know the most likely candidate for a disciple maker is the man in his seventies. I wouldn't have selected him either. The truth is these are two real guys, and one gets it and the other hasn't yet.

The point here is really very simple. The person who becomes a disciple maker is not always who you think it will be. Some people catch it, and some don't. You never know who will, so you should never, ever overlook taking the time to explain disciple making to someone. Even after you have spent a significant amount of time with someone, he or she might still drop the ball on multiplying. Equip them anyway.

What makes some people "get it" and others lag behind? I think it comes down to two things—the Truth of God, and the Spirit of God. When the Holy Spirit brings a person to an understanding of God's truth, life change is going to happen. It does not matter who you are, where you are from, or what you have done. When God reveals His truth into your mind and the Spirit prompts your heart, change is on the horizon.

My seventy-year-old friend is a perfect example of how someone "gets it." This man knows more Bible than most people have forgotten in a lifetime. However, when he recently began to see the way Christ multiplied disciples, the Holy Spirit started giving him a conviction he had not previously had. For years he has had a conviction about the theology of Christ's life, and now he has a conviction about the methodology of Christ's life.

My young seminary friend, on the other hand, has just not gotten the vision for a life of personal multiplication. It is not because he ignores Scripture; he reads his Bible regularly. It is not because the Holy Spirit is not within him; he is filled with God's Spirit. He just has not yet been convicted by the Spirit of the truth in his life regarding his personal responsibility for fulfilling the Great Commission. Hopefully, in time, he will be convicted by the Spirit about the truth he has in his mind. Like me, and maybe even you, hopefully he will come to a place of conviction about reproducing disciples.

Near the end of His days, Jesus was praying to the Father for His disciples. Here is what He prayed in John 17:17, *"Sanctify them by the truth; Your word is truth."* Jesus was asking the Father to set apart His disciples by the truth of His Word. Being set apart by the truth makes the difference between those who get it and those who don't. Speak the truth to everyone, and trust God to make the unlikely into the likely.

Day Eighty-Four:
"Being and Building Lacrosse Players"

Over the past three years I have witnessed a very unusual example of disciple making; I have seen a movement of disciples of the sport of lacrosse. I live in a county outside of Atlanta, Georgia that has a population of about 115,000. I have lived in this county for almost 18 years and have watched it grow from about 50,000 to the current population.

Until three years ago, this county had not one active lacrosse team playing the sport. I don't even think a local sporting goods store carried one piece of lacrosse equipment. In all the years I have lived in this county, I have never even heard anybody mention the sport of lacrosse.

Today it is a different story. All three high schools in our county have club teams that play lacrosse. The local YMCA has started a youth league that has grown into four major divisions and now has several hundred kids, including my son, playing lacrosse games every Saturday. Every major sporting goods store now sells lacrosse equipment, and people are talking about it everywhere you go.

This surge of lacrosse players in our small suburban county is primarily the result of Tom who moved here from Buffalo, New York and works for the local YMCA. Tom played lacrosse in college and has been addicted ever since. His passion for the game is contagious.

Every Saturday I sit on the sidelines of a lacrosse game watching Tom walk around the fields checking on the games. I am continually impressed with the way this one man has single-handedly built a movement of athletes and coaches who are learning how to be and build lacrosse players. Tom has taken his mission very seriously and has been extremely successful. I think I can safely say that if Tom left our town, the sport of lacrosse would live on!

Wow! Do you see what I am driving at? Has the point hit you? Have the dots connected yet?

Tom has done for the sport of lacrosse what God has commanded us to do with the Gospel of Jesus Christ. Like Tom, we need to be contagious about making disciples. We need to channel our efforts into teaching others how to live as disciples of Christ and how to lead others to live as disciples. We need to live our lives in such a way that disciples of Christ would continue to be made even if we had to move somewhere else.

Playing lacrosse has some great benefits such as physical exercise and teaching teamwork. Watching a game is fun, and both guys and girls can play. It's easy to see why lacrosse is catching on in our county.

Being a disciple of Christ has some great benefits as well. Discipleship is good for the soul and can make our lives better. The quality of our earthly and eternal life is greatly improved because of the time spent investing in others. Living for Christ is a blast and is a life available to men, women, boys, and girls. If being and building players of lacrosse is catching on, how much more should being and building disciples of Christ be catching on?

May Acts 14:21 become true for where we all live, *"They preached the good news in that city and won a large number of disciples."*

Day Eighty-Five:
"The Forward Life"

Until a few years ago the word "forward" rarely came up in
conversation. When the word "forward" did come up, it usually meant
the position a basketball or hockey player occupied. Today, I see the
word "forward" almost every day of my life. E-mail has made the
concept of forwarding messages a common occurrence. Just about every
hour of the day someone sends me a message that they received from
someone else. Many times I return the favor by clicking the forward
button on my computer and passing the message on to others.

Just about everybody I talk to has different feelings about the
forwarding of e-mails. Some people hate getting forwarded messages
and delete them immediately. Others enjoy the forwarding capabilities
of their computer and they enjoy the exchange of meaningless messages
throughout the day. I wonder how many hours of work time are wasted
by the exchange of forwards throughout the day.

This fairly recent phenomenon of forwarding e-mails has raised
some interesting questions for me. Why has forwarding e-mails become
so captivating? Why is it almost addicting to some people while others
despise it? Why are people so willing to give so much time to forwarding
meaningless information? I often sit at my computer and wonder who
thinks up some of the stuff that crosses my computer screen.

Why on earth are so many people willing to forward meaningless
messages on e-mail and yet not the least bit concerned with forwarding
the message of Jesus Christ by making disciples? I wonder what the
world might be like if we spent more of our time in a small group
making disciples rather than in front of our computers forwarding e-
mails. If making disciples were as easy as clicking a button, would we
be more likely to do it? Do we shy away from making disciples because
of the hard work that it involves? Is looking at a computer screen taking
the place of looking someone in the eyes and communicating the life-
changing message of Jesus? What would happen if we were as emotional
about the Great Commission as we are about receiving forwarded
messages? Sadly, I don't know very many people who have an addiction
for the Great Commission!

The point is simple. Why do we get caught up in so many things of the world and have such a hard time staying obedient to the Word? Have we forgotten that obedience pleases the Father? Have we forgotten that when we do what Jesus did that is a life of obedience? In John 8:29 Jesus said, *"The One who sent Me is with Me; He has not left Me alone, for I always do what pleases Him."*

So, how about you? Are you doing what pleases the Father? Are you forwarding the Great Commandment and the Great Commission? Are you making disciples who pass on to others what you have given to them?

My challenge is every time you see a forward in your inbox and every time you click the forward button on the taskbar, you would remember your mission in life is to make disciples who make disciples. In other words, live a "forward" life.

Day Eighty-Six:
"The Making of Disciple Makers"

In the past year, God has given me another opportunity to have
a front-row seat in watching Him mold a group of men into disciple
makers.

It all started as God began to surface a handful of men in my life
who had a desire for more. Brooks, Rich, Billy, and three men named
Jeff are all men that I had relationships with from our weekend crowd at
church or the small couples group I attended. The common denominator
in this group was "desire." Each man had a desire to grow deeper with
God and a willingness to stay committed to a discipleship group for a
year in order to experience another level of growth.

These six men and I met consistently once a week for the better part
of a year. We had a couple of other men join us for part of the journey,
but these six men stayed the course. The course was not particularly
easy either. Our meeting time was on Sunday afternoons at 4:00. That
is not the prime-time meeting hour for any group, much less a group of
guys who would love to do a hundred other things on Sunday afternoons.
Prime time or not, we met each week to do three things—learn together,
pray together, and hold each other accountable.

During the weekly meetings, we used the Impact Discipleship
curriculum, but the curriculum was not the key ingredient for our
growth. The key ingredients for growth were the Spirit of God and the
Word of God. I have come to realize that any curriculum that helps get
people in the Word of God is a good curriculum. We used Impact for two
reasons. First, I'm partial to the materials that I've written. The second
reason is the curriculum is based on the life of Christ. I can think of no
better way to make disciples than by studying the Master disciple maker.

In the course of our weekly meetings, several important things took
place. One was life transformation. Right before my very eyes I watched
a group of men be transformed by the truth of God and the Spirit of God.
I saw men's values about marriage, family, money, and ministry change
over the course of a year. I watched them go on mission trips and step up
to be small group leaders and servants within the ministry of our church.
I watched these men say things about the Scriptures that they had never
said before in their lives. I watched them learn to share their faith and

pray like they had never done before. Watching God transform a life is amazing and never gets old.

Something else that happened during our time together was the building of community. Our level of friendship goes deeper than most church relationships. We are not all "best" friends, but there is a sense of camaraderie among the guys in this group that will last for years. When people laugh together and share deep feelings together, a bond develops that makes us a spiritual family.

One other thing that happened in this group was a sharpening through accountability. We did not always ask each other questions for accountability, but we always had a sense of accountability. Just knowing the other men would be there and ready to meet was accountability itself. The accountability questions we did ask were simply bonus points for the process of sharpening our lives.

After meeting together for a full year, we made a decision that would radically change our nice little men's group. We made the decision to include others! The decision to include others meant expanding into multiple groups which meant changing the dynamic of our group. We knew the minute we expanded into other groups that our group would never be the same, but we expanded anyway!

We expanded our group because it was the right thing to do. We didn't expand because everyone was ready to lead. We didn't expand because there was pressure to meet certain goals. We didn't expand because we were tired of each other and wanted something new. We expanded because that's what Jesus told us to do.

This small group of men did not learn everything there is to know about being a disciple in the course of a year. They have learned enough to know how to keep growing and how to help others grow. We decided it was time to multiply. Some of the men paired up and began new groups together. A few of the men partnered with other men who are committed to multiplying. Already, these men have done what few Christians will ever do: they have made other disciples. I'm still sitting on the front row watching God work, but I know that these men are not just disciples, they are disciple makers.

Day Eighty-Seven:
"If Not Now, When?"

Has anyone ever given you a "round-to-it"? It is a small wooden coin with the words "round-to-it" printed on the side. Obviously, the idea is that there are some things we are only going to do when we get *around to it*.

Sadly, some people have a round-to-it attitude toward the priority of making disciples who make disciples. They know what Jesus did and what He told us to do. They simply have not made the very thing Jesus came to do a priority in their own lives.

I'm not sure how that happens. How can we not make time to do the very thing Jesus came to do? How on earth do we claim to follow a man who came to "make disciples" and not make one disciple our entire lives?

I can literally count on two hands the number of people I know who have taken seriously Christ's command to multiply their lives. These are people who have decided not to wait to make disciples. They have gotten around to it and are making disciples who will impact generations to come.

As I look at the proven disciple makers I know, there are several things I notice about their lives that have made disciple making a reality.

First, they have grasped the proper vision. Many people never get around to making disciples because they suffer from blurred vision. They have never been clearly shown that the life Christ lived was one that reproduced other disciples. Jesus stated it so clearly in John 20:21, *"As the Father has sent Me, I am sending you."*

Second, they have the correct knowledge. I am amazed at how many people I talk to about disciple making who say, "I've been going to church all my life and never heard anything about multiplying disciples." How on earth can the church not be committed to teaching the very thing Christ was doing? We need to realize that people will never make time for disciple making if they have never been taught to do it.

Third, they make it a priority. Let's be honest. You do what you want to do, don't you? I wrote this book because I made it a priority in my life. I have plenty of other things to do with my time, but I got around to writing this book because it was a priority in my life. Many Christians never make a disciple because they never make disciple making a priority in their lives.

A fourth thing I have noticed is that proven disciple makers choose to live in obedience to Christ's command. When Jesus says, *"Make disciples of all nations,"* they do it. They do not make excuses, they just do it.

Finally, proven multipliers are busy about the right things. The disciple-making barrier I hear the most is, "I'm just too busy!" Listen, if you are too busy to do what Jesus did, you are just too busy. We are all busy, but we need to be busy about the right things. Do not get so busy with "good" things that you miss out on doing the "best" things.

So, how about you? When are you going to get around to it? What is your excuse for not doing the very thing Jesus came to do? If you do not make disciples, when will you?

Day Eighty-Eight:
"If Not You, Who?"

Just the other day, I was in a meeting with several potential leaders in our church. We were having a discussion about the qualifications of a leader within our church when a woman in the group said, "I know I have some gifts, I just don't have the gift for evangelism and disciple making."

Obviously, the lady in our group had the right heart, but she also had the wrong understanding. She clearly misunderstood that sharing Christ with people and making disciples of all nations is not a task reserved for people with a certain "gift." Sharing Christ and making disciples is a command for everyone who claims to be a Christ follower.

This woman represents the way many Christians think about the process of multiplying disciples. I can't tell you how many people I have met who think making disciples is a job for an elite group of believers. I've met others who think only pastors can make disciples. I have met people who think only people with seminary training can make disciples. I have talked to people who think disciple making is only for people with the gift of teaching or the gift of leadership.

What a tragic mistake to think that the process of making disciples is a task set aside for only a handful of believers. How could we possibly fulfill Christ's commission to make disciples of *"all nations"* if we limited the *"teaching them to obey"* part of disciple making to a small percentage of followers?

In order to make disciples of all nations, we need all-hands-on-deck. We need a movement of multiplying disciples that is made up of Great Commandment and Great Commission Christians—not just trained professionals. As far as I know, the most important qualification for disciple making is great passion! If we have a movement of people with great passion who are committed to living out the Great Commandment and Great Commission, we will see great results for the greatest Kingdom of all—Christ's Kingdom!

Think of it like this. We live in a world filled with people who ride bicycles. Everyone who rides a bike was most likely taught to ride by someone else. The teacher was the person who ran beside the bike countless times until the rider was able to ride without help. My guess is that most of the people who teach people to ride bikes have the following qualifications: First, they know how to ride a bike. Second, they are willing to help others learn to ride a bike. Third, they passionately care about seeing the person they are training learn how to ride a bike.

Teaching a person to ride a bike is not limited to professional bicycle riders. Teaching a person to ride a bike is not a job only for people who own bike shops. Teaching a person to ride a bike is not just for people named Schwinn. The bottom line is—anyone who rides a bike can teach another person to ride a bike! By the way, if you teach them well, they can go on and teach others. If you don't watch out, you might start a whole movement of bike riders and teachers. You might have people teaching and riding bikes all over the world.

If you don't make a disciple who makes a disciple, who will?

Day Eighty-Nine:
"If Not Here, Where?"

A restaurant owner in a small town opens his doors each Tuesday night, when the restaurant is officially closed, to host a group of people meeting for discipleship.

A car dealer makes a room in his showroom available for employees to gather each week for a discipleship meeting.

A lady invites fellow teachers into her principal's office after school hours to meet together for prayer and Bible study.

A fitness center manager meets with a couple of guys each week for discipleship after the club closes.

A man who owns a plumbing business uses a room in his shop to meet with guys he is discipling.

I could go on and on with my list of places where I know people have demonstrated a commitment to the process of making disciples who make disciples. I can't actually verify it, but my hunch is those places that have been used for disciple making are probably places that have experienced the Lord's favor. At least I know the Lord promises to be with us *"always, to the very end of the age"* if we live out the commission He gave us to make disciples.

As cool as it is for disciple making to be taking place in a bunch of different places, I think it is very sad that it doesn't take place as often as it should within the walls of the local church. Please don't misunderstand what I am saying. I think it is a great thing to see disciple making taking place outside of the church. I believe that is exactly what Christ wants. My only concern is that some of the people I know who are doing disciple making outside of their church are doing so because no one is emphasizing it inside their church.

I think we need to be making disciples all over the place, but I think it ought to originate from within the church. I have actually had people tell me that their pastor was against them starting a discipleship group with people in their church. I know of one church that had over one hundred men in discipleship groups and asked them to stop meeting while the church did a program for about six weeks. The program was a good thing, but the discipleship effort was squelched and never encouraged to start back.

I have a hard time understanding how church leadership can't see the church being a place where disciple making is encouraged, taught, and promoted. In fact, I have a difficult time understanding how church leaders are not the ones setting the example. Maybe that is the problem. A pastor is not likely to promote something that he doesn't live out.

Ephesians 4:11-12 tells us that Christ *"gave some...to be pastors and teachers, to prepare God's people for works of service, so that the body of Christ may be built up..."* I believe those verses make it clear that the role of a pastor is to equip or prepare God's people for ministry. What better way to do that than to lead the church to be a training center. Isn't that what Jesus did? Jesus prepared His disciples to do ministry, then let them do it.

As I see it, disciple making ought to happen anywhere and everywhere, but it should begin in the church. The church should be like the beginning point of a ripple in a pond. What began in a local church ought to ripple out to *"every nation."*

Day Ninety:
"Are You Willing to Die?"

Inside every seed is a forest, not a tree!

What a powerful statement. Every seed has within it the potential to reproduce a whole forest of trees. Just think about that. One single tree is filled with seeds that can fall to the ground, take root in the soil, and bloom into a full grown tree which drop seeds to the ground that become even more trees. That is what we call the "cycle of life." Isn't it amazing that God made His creation the way He did?

There is only one problem when it comes to growing a forest from a single seed. The seed must die! That's right; the seed must die to produce life. In John 12:24 Jesus says, *"I tell you the truth, unless a kernel of wheat falls to the ground and dies, it remains only a single seed. But if it dies, it produces many seeds."*

The fitting question for you on the last lesson of this book is, "Are you willing to die?"

Are you willing to die to yourself and your wishes so that other disciples can be made and reproduced? Are you willing to set aside your own personal agenda so that God's agenda can be carried out in your life? Are you willing to spend the rest of your life consistently investing in a handful of disciples who have the potential to become an entire forest of disciples?

I want to leave you with an encouragement to die! That's right. I am encouraging you to make the decision to die to yourself and give yourself to what Christ gave His life to. Christ gave His life to make possible a movement of multiplying disciples that could take His message to every nation, tongue, and tribe. If Christ had not been willing to die, I wouldn't be writing this book, and you wouldn't be reading it. Everything as we know it would be different.

So how will your life's story be told? Will it be said of you that you gave your life to that which Christ gave His? Will it be said of you that your willingness to die brought life to thousands? Will it be said that you were a seed that was willing to die to become a forest?

I once heard a story about a missionary who was headed into a tribal area that meant certain death. As he boarded the boat to set sail for this area, his loved ones pleaded with him not to go. They cried out, "Please don't go; you will never come back. You will die."

His response was amazing. He said, "You don't understand, I am already dead."

I can only imagine the angels in heaven telling Jesus He would die if He came to earth and Jesus responding that He already had. Jesus' life was a seed that has produced a forest. I am a tree that has life because He died. How many more trees will have life because I am willing to die? How many trees will have life because you are willing to die?

Can you hear Jesus saying, *"Come and die with me"*?

MINISTRY INFORMATION

Impact Discipleship Ministries exists to help people and churches be and build disciples of Jesus Christ. Please go to our website at impactdisciples.com to find out more information, shop more of our products, and connect with us.

Contact information:
impactdisciples.com
(678) 854-9322
2564 HWY 154
Newnan, GA
30265

Made in the USA
Columbia, SC
09 March 2019